"The Western church desperately needs conversations around what local church activities look like in light of the gospel of the kingdom: pastoring, outreach, worship, teaching and forming people spiritually. Kent and Mike have done the hard work of thinking about and living these things, helping the rest of us know where to start and what to do."

JAN JOHNSON, author of *Spiritual Disciplines Companion* and *Invitation to the Jesus Life*

"The release of *Renovation of the Church* is a bright day for the church. Carlson and Lueken offer a wonderfully candid, bold book about the journey of a church that stopped appealing to religious consumers and started producing disciples of Jesus."

GARY W. MOON, executive director, Renovaré Institute for Christian Spiritual Formation

"This book is a breath of fresh air that brings with it the aroma of hope—hope that maybe, just maybe, there's a different way to do this thing we call church. But more than just a different *way*, Mike and Kent began with a different *desire*—a desire to be part of a community of faith that was characterized by something beyond success, a community that would actually begin to resemble the character and fragrance of Christ. Their journey toward fulfilling that desire has been a long and difficult one—costly too! But if you're like me, you'll find it full . . . of hope."

DAVID JOHNSON, senior pastor, Church of the Open Door, Minneapolis

"Bold, courageous, humorous and refreshingly honest! Carlson and Lueken invite us into a journey that few churches would ever attempt—shifting their church from a 'consumer driven' church model to a 'disciple-making' church model (a novel idea!). *Renovation of the Church* is a must-read for every pastor, church leader or seminarian who longs to see the church fulfill the heart of its mission!"

KEITH J. MATTHEWS, professor, Graduate School of Theology, Azusa Pacific University

"I do not know of a church that has more thoroughly applied what Renovaré cares about to an entire congregation than Oak Hills Church in Folsom, California. Read this book to help your church catalyze the kingdom life of God that is within us and between us."

LYLE SMITH GRAYBEAL, coordinator, Renovaré USA

"The honest story of two courageous pastors who dared to change the ethos of their church from a membership focus to a discipleship focus, from catering to consumers to creating Christ followers. Their story will inspire you."

JAMES BRYAN SMITH, author of *The Good and Beautiful God*

FOREWORD BY DALLAS WILLARD

RENOVATION
of the CHURCH

WHAT HAPPENS WHEN A SEEKER CHURCH

DISCOVERS SPIRITUAL FORMATION

KENT CARLSON *and* MIKE LUEKEN

IVP Books

An imprint of InterVarsity Press
Downers Grove, Illinois

InterVarsity Press
P.O. Box 1400, Downers Grove, IL 60515-1426
World Wide Web: www.ivpress.com
E-mail: email@ivpress.com

InterVarsity Press® is the book-publishing division of InterVarsity Christian Fellowship/USA®, a movement of students and faculty active on campus at hundreds of universities, colleges and schools of nursing in the United States of America, and a member movement of the International Fellowship of Evangelical Students. For information about local and regional activities, write Public Relations Dept., InterVarsity Christian Fellowship/USA, 6400 Schroeder Rd., P.O. Box 7895, Madison, WI 53707-7895, or visit the IVCF website at <www.intervarsity.org>.

All Scripture quotations, unless otherwise indicated, are taken from the Holy Bible, Today's New International Version™ Copyright © 2001 by International Bible Society. All rights reserved.

While all stories in this book are true, some names and identifying information in this book have been changed to protect the privacy of the individuals involved.

Parts of chapter six, "Setting Aside Ambition," first appeared as "Pastoral Ambition: Does Success Chip Away at Our Souls?" Out of Ur, October 3, 2006 <www.outofur.com/archives/2006/10/pastoral_ambiti.html#more>. Used by permission.

Design: Cindy Kiple
Images: pomegranate: Jonathan Kantor/Getty Images
         pomegranates: Joe Clark/Getty Images

ISBN 978-0-8308-3546-1

Printed in the United States of America ∞

Library of Congress Cataloging-in-Publication Data

Carlson, Kent, 1954-
  Renovation of the Church: what happens when a seeker church
discovers spiritual formation/Kent Carlson and Mike Lueken.
     p. cm.
  Includes bibliographical references.
  ISBN 978-0-8308-3546-1 (pbk.: alk. paper)
  1. Spiritual formation. 2. Oak Hills Church (Folsom, Calif.) I.
Lueken, Mike, 1964- II. Title.
  BV4511.C26 2011
  253—dc22

2010052962

| P | 18 | 17 | 16 | 15 | 14 | 13 | 12 | 11 | 10 | 9 | 8 | 7 | 6 | 5 | 4 | 3 | 2 | 1 |
| Y | 25 | 24 | 23 | 22 | 21 | 20 | 19 | 18 | 17 | 16 | 15 | 14 | 13 | 12 | 11 | | | |

To our wives:

Diane and Julie

Our journey at Oak Hills has been

carried lovingly in your hearts,

and we are deeply grateful for

your constant and unwavering

belief and support

CONTENTS

FOREWORD

*H*ow do we present the radical message of Christ in a church that has catered to the religious demands of the nominally committed? In other words, if we have gathered people into congregations by appeasing their appetites and desires, how can we help them deal with the fact that their problems in life and character—even "in church"—are primarily caused by living to get what they want? How can the cross and self-denial become the central fact in a prosperous, consumer culture? How can discipleship to Jesus—in a sense recognizable from the Bible, with the spiritual transformation it brings—be the mode of operation in a thriving North American congregation?

Kent Carlson and Mike Lueken, pastors of Oak Hills Church near Sacramento, California, answer this question—the single most important question in the church culture of North America today. They do that by telling the story of how they interacted with God, along with loving and courageous members of their congregation, to *actually do it*. It is first of all a story of how they personally came to grips with the dynamics of a large "attractional" congregation widely viewed as very successful. They found that "we [in the dominant form of church life today] have trained Christians to be demanding consumers, not disciples." "It was this issue of consumerism that brought the conflicting values of external success and authentic spiritual formation into such sharp contrast."

But the dynamics of outward success in a church are rooted in the motivational forces of the pastors and leaders. These have to change before anything else does. The pastors must themselves become disciples (in the New Testament sense), genuinely becoming in their concrete existence, their life and relationships, what we see repeatedly depicted in well-known biblical passages. It is personal ambition that drives the machinery of "success" in the church context, which is what comes out in the many dimensions of character failure that now are all too familiar. Often church members are caught up in their desire to be associated with a "successful" church. Among the treasures expressed in this book is, "Christian leaders are more ready to be candid about sexual lust than ambition." But lust fulfilled is only one dimension of the deeper drive to *have my way*. The deeper root of consumerism in the church context is sensuality.

When that root has been cut in the individual life, then genuine ambition for God, and pride in the cross, can flourish (Galatians 6:14). The power of God can then flow through transformed character into a world desperate for it. Success is redefined by the spread of kingdom presence throughout the community. Church growth is not just more Christians but bigger Christians, flush with Christ's character.

The co-pastors of Oak Hills Church came to know this through their own personal growth together—often in the travail and tumult of congregational processes and the pain of radical authenticity between them. They came very practically to know and to rest in what it means for Christ to be in charge—not abstractly and in theory, but concretely, with real people and events, "warts and all." Another amazing insight is that "it is spiritually formative to be dissatisfied and unable to resolve it." That is the prime location of faith and grace, building character.

The authors came to grips with major issues for practice—for what we actually must *do* if we intend to make the Great Commission of Matthew 28:18-20 into the mission statement of our group. First, we must *intend* to do that, and must lead our people into that intention. And our central message—our "gospel"—must be one that has a natural tendency to produce *disciples* of Jesus, not just avid consumers of religious goods and services. Disciples are self-starters in kingdom living, on the road with Jesus day in and day out. The gospel of life now in the present kingdom of the heavens (Matthew 4:17) will produce disciples. And then we organize our "meetings," of whatever kind, around that intention and that message. We set the meetings up in a way that intelligently develops disciples and fosters their progressive transformation into Christlikeness from the inside. Careful attention to the Spirit, the Bible and how experience actually moves in individuals and groups will enable us to do this. It has been done repeatedly in Christian history, and can be done now. Outwardly, in fact, our operation may not look much different than it does now. But its content, its goal and its outcome will most assuredly bring the people involved into a path of contemporary holiness that looks at Matthew 5–7, 1 Corinthians 13 and Colossians 3:1-17, and says: "Of course. That's us." Grace with training in fellowship will bring us there.

The authors would be the first to tell us that they have not "arrived" or have it all worked out. Indeed, as they clearly indicate, it just is not that kind of thing. But they understand the glory and goodness of Paul's practice: "I press on toward the goal to win the prize for which God has called me heavenward in Christ Jesus" (Philippians 3:14). They know this is not inspirational verbiage or only for spiritual oddities, but a statement of realism for church life. Anyone can carry this out, because God certainly will enable those who intend it. They will learn how as they go, because they have a Teacher who is faithful. Who is "with you always." Really.

Kent Carlson and Mike Lueken love the church—not an abstract one but the one that meets here and there, down on the corner or in a warehouse. They love *their* church. They know that there is absolutely nothing wrong with the church—those that meet—which discipleship and intelligent intention toward Christlikeness cannot more than fix. Anyone who is concerned to break the grip of un-Christlike Christianity on the church visible today, or on themselves, has only to "follow their example as they follow Christ" (see 1 Corinthians 11:1). Please read this book and creatively apply it to your situation, with the Teacher beside you. You don't need more money or new facilities. Just begin where you are and all else will take care of itself. No, God will take care of it.

Dallas Willard

INTRODUCTION

KENT CARLSON

&

*H*i there. We're new to the area, and we're looking for a new church home. We found your website and were wondering if you could answer a few questions about your church." On the surface this begins a conversation repeated countless times every week in the religious life of North America. This family has a decision to make, and they are trying to make it in the only way they know how. They have a list of wants and desires that they hope a church can fulfill, and they are doing some comparison shopping. Out of the various churches in the area, they are trying to find the one that most closely aligns with them.

It's a big deal for a family to find a church. It can be an unsettling time. The reasons for looking for a new church home varies from person to person. This may be a new beginning for them, and they may want to get involved in a church for the first time, perhaps in decades. They may be looking for a church that is similar to the one they came from. On the other hand, they may be coming out of a difficult church situation and are looking for one that is opposite of the church they left. They may be wondering if our church has a denominational affiliation or what style of worship we have. They may be interested in our youth or our children's ministry. Their priorities may be doctrinal, political or simply practical ("Do you have an early service, because we like to take our boat out on the lake on Sundays?"). And sometimes they want to find out, although it is unlikely they will say it this way, if they can meet God here.

Underneath it all, though, there is something going on that makes all this rather complicated and messy, and, from our perspective, exposes some core difficulties about church life today. This family innocently approaches our church as consumers, and I, in turn, respond as a provider of religious goods. It is my job to present our various "products" in such a way that this family will be inclined to choose us over the religious offerings of the other churches in town. There is a weirdness to this. I've never gotten used to it. I know it is the way the game is played, and I have no ideal alternative as to how it might be played differently, but I can't help but feel that there is something fundamentally flawed about the whole thing.

Eventually, someone looking for a church home will ask some variation of this question: "So, what kind of church are you?" Such an easy question to ask, but I don't think it is a very easy question to answer. I don't know how to describe a church in a short telephone conversation. Actually, I don't think I know how to describe almost anything of substance in a short telephone conversation. It's like someone asking me, "What kind of a family do you have?" How would I answer that? Would I talk about the house we live in, the cars we drive, the various things we have accomplished, the jobs we have, the investments we have made? I suspect not. I think I would begin by telling some of the stories of our family. I'd talk about some of the big moments, the tragedies, the celebrations, the milestones, the disappointments, the mistakes. I'd also tell some of the hilarious and absurd moments, as well as some of the quiet, poignant moments that can almost capture the heart of my family.

In a sense, that is what Mike and I are trying to do in this book.

THE STORY OF A CHURCH

This book is a story about a church. It is written from the perspective of two pastors who have lived and struggled in the midst of it. We write not as theorists but as practitioners. We are telling this story not as historians but as "evangelists." We write about good news, wonderful news. We write to inspire. To challenge. Perhaps even to incite a rebellion. We dream of another way of being the church. We dare to hope that this dream captures others as well.

We write for two reasons. First, in spite of wonderful stories of outward success and church growth, we believe that the church in North America is in serious trouble. We know there are voices in the church today who disagree with this assessment. Some even go so far as to point to the rise of the megachurch and other external successes as indicators of a robust Christianity on the move. We respectfully disagree.

If church leaders believe that the church in North America is healthy and is merely experiencing troubles that have typically plagued the church through the centuries, then they will gently tweak existing structures and programs, or perhaps simply add to what is already happening. In other words, if the patient is not sick, nobody will look for a cure. We believe the patient is indeed desperately sick and needs to recover from a religious system that places a premium on outward success. We add our voices to the growing number of those inside and outside the church who are calling for the church to be reformed. We Christian leaders have created the current religious system, or at least have been complicit in its flourishing, and we ought to feel a responsibility for the rather meager and impotent product that has resulted. An important and messy dialogue on these issues is required of us. This book is an attempt to lend our voices to that dialogue.

Yet in no way do we believe that we are getting everything right. Quite to the contrary, we spend many of our days wondering if we are getting *anything* right. Some days we find ourselves looking at our church as a laboratory, and we're desperately trying to keep the laboratory open so we can keep the experiments in spiritual formation going. Some days, after another failed experiment leaves us with broken beakers and smudged faces in a smoke-filled room, we try to find the motivation to clean up the place and start over again. This book is not another success story. We're not convinced we know how to do it. We offer neither a seven-step strategy to reform the church nor five key principles for success. We are simply dissatisfied with the state of the church in North America, repentant over our part in it and determined to find another way. This book is about that journey.

The second reason we are writing this book is less dramatic, but no less important for us: we hope this story will benefit the people of Oak Hills Church. When we unplugged from the high-octane, entrepreneurial, pragmatic, success-driven, attractional model of church growth, our church was plunged into a decade-long roller-coaster ride of excessive (at times) introspection, organizational upheaval, uncertainty, plummeting attendance and fractured relationships. Sadly, a certain percentage of this was due to our own mistakes and internal and philosophical angst. We struggled with how to restructure the DNA of our church without ruining the church in the process. It has been a costly journey. Well over a thousand people left our church for other churches in the area. Many of those people had poured years of work and resources into the ministry. It hurt to lose them. We know it harmed many of them as well.

The larger story though, and the one we want to emphasize here, is that many stayed and struggled with us. Many others joined us in the midst of this story. Others, wonderfully, have returned. We are thankful for all of them. We continue to dream together of doing church another way. In good times and bad, through seasons of confusion and clarity, hundreds of people have refused to give up and have demonstrated in countless ways their support, trust and belief that God was and is up to something. They have embraced the Benedictine vow of stability. They have pushed back at the cultural norm of viewing the church as consumers, a place to get their spiritual needs met. Their loyalty and long obedience in the same direction is a constant source of encouragement and a powerful motivator to stay faithful to our calling as pastors. We are extremely grateful for them. This story is largely their story, and we wanted to write it so that they would know the story and understand their place in it.

THE SHAPE OF THE BOOK

The first three chapters of this book comprise a quick overview of the story of our church. This story is told with an emphasis on explaining the tumultuous transition that began around the year 2000. In truth, there is nothing that fascinating, or at least unique, about our church before this. We were riding the same religious and cultural wave that brought relative outward success to thousands of suburban churches during that time. But our story since then has been somewhat unique, and while it is still fresh in our minds, we want to tell it.

The greater portion of this book, though, is an attempt to take some of the larger, overarching themes and "learnings" we have stumbled upon and flesh them out in greater detail. Some of these themes overwhelmed us like flashes of lightening. Other themes snuck up on us gradually, and only after the fact, upon careful reflection, have we noticed their power and influence on us. Regardless, these have become some of the core values that brought about and shaped our church in the past decade. While this section of the book will be more objective and propositional, we hope you will be able to see the intricate connection these themes have with our story.

There is something else you should know. Relentless authenticity is a huge value at Oak Hills. We are aware that this does not make us at all unique. In fact, you would have to search pretty diligently to find a church that didn't say it values authenticity these days. Yet we believe it is common for people to be more drawn to the concept of authenticity than the thing itself. There remain many in our world who do not enjoy being confronted with the raw truth about themselves or others. Many of us enjoy our truth in neat and tidy packages that do not disturb us too greatly. For good or for bad, our story is neither neat nor tidy, and it would not be in keeping with who we are to pretty it up or put an overly polite or religious veneer on it.

Mike and I are pastors. We tenaciously believe in the church. Even in our most cynical and despairing days we still had this sense that the church is the bride of Christ and is therefore precious to him. Even when we wanted to quit and be butchers, or spend our days in the bleachers of Wrigley Field, or do almost anything other than work in a church, we found that we could not walk away from Christ's bride. In many ways this book is our attempt to express our stubborn love for the church in general and Oak Hills Church specifically.

1

THE CREATION OF
THE MONSTER

KENT CARLSON

*O*ak Hills Church began with seventeen people on a Sunday morning in November 1984. We had rented space in a strip mall in the heart of the quickly growing but still quaint little suburb known as Folsom. For a number of weeks I walked Folsom's streets, going door to door, inviting people to this brand new church. I hated it. I can't think of a person who came to our church because of all that door knocking. But it was all I knew how to do. Finally, a number of young families from another church visited us, and we began to grow slowly from there.

Almost everyone in the church joined a small group of some kind. Whenever we had a party or some sort of an event, almost everybody attended, and there was a sense throughout the church that something very good was happening. I had no particular philosophy of church planting, an intentional strategy of outreach or even a well-developed theology of the church. I just had a rather vague interest in leading a community of people who wanted to learn how to follow Christ together and live fully. Those were very enjoyable and deeply rewarding days.

We were young and everyone shouldered the responsibility of leading. The leadership team of this small church met every week for four hours. We went on two leadership retreats a year. We had regular poker and cigar nights. We all played on a softball team together. We took vacations together. We simply enjoyed hanging out with each other. And the church grew slowly.

By 1990 there were close to two hundred people coming to Oak Hills, but there was a sense among the church leadership that something was not quite right. Most of the people in our church had come from other churches. This was not bad in itself because the majority of them had recently moved into the area. But we had not seen many new believers become a part of our church. Like most churches, one of our stated purposes, one of the reasons we existed, was to reach people who were outside the family of God. We simply admitted to ourselves that we were doing a lousy job of this.

THE WILLOW CREEK EXPERIENCE

While we were discussing all of this, the phenomenon of Willow Creek Community Church, in South Barrington, Illinois, was bursting on the church-growth scene. Willow Creek had spent the 1980s orienting its church around reaching nonchurched people by the thousands through their seeker-targeted services, and the world was taking notice. I had a very good friend who was intimately involved with Willow, and he kept telling me I had to come to one of Willow's church leadership conferences. So in October 1990, seven us from Oak Hills (affectionately referred to in Oak Hills Church lore as the Chicago Seven) hopped on a plane and spent a week at Willow.

We sat through four days of one of the most inspiring events I had ever attended. We were in awe of the facilities, the professionalism, the music, the dramatic sketches, the multimedia, the messages and the Chicago-style deep-dish pizza. But there was a moment at one of the sessions that remains the most memorable for me. Bill Hybels, the founding pastor and visionary architect of the Willow movement, was speaking. His message was simple, believable, convicting and highly motivating. He asked a very straightforward question: "If lost people matter to God, then why don't they matter to you?"

I can still remember the moment when Hybels said those words. I was leaning forward on the edge of my seat with my head in my hands and tears in my eyes. I remember vowing at that moment that if God allowed me to remain as the pastor of Oak Hills, I would do everything in my power to reorient our church around reaching lost people. And then I just raised my head an inch or so and looked down the row at my six friends, and each was sitting in the same way, edge of the seat, leaning forward, head in their hands. We caught each other's eyes and knew that something had happened. We got it. We were hooked. As we gathered in the evening in our hotel, we made plans, we prayed, we dreamed, and we began to prepare ourselves for the adventure ahead.

BRINGING WILLOW CREEK TO FOLSOM

Since 1988 our church had been meeting on Sunday afternoons at another local church. It was the only place large enough in Folsom that we could afford. We knew that Sunday afternoons were less than ideal to begin new seeker-targeted services, so we decided to begin a Saturday night service. These began in the spring of 1991, and those were wonderful and exciting days.

One of my many failed majors in college was theater, so the production and performance aspect of the Willow model was great fun for me. It was right in my sweet spot. Every week we had the challenge of putting together and performing an hour-long theatrical production. We had great music, intriguing dramatic sketches, engaging testimonies and sermons that—as it often said in our brochures and periodic community postcards—wouldn't put you to sleep. We came up with a slogan that became a byline in almost every piece of literature we published: Oak Hills Church—You'll Be Surprised!

For the first time in our church's history we had a philosophy of outreach that was both intentional and effective. This was part of the pragmatic genius of the Willow model in those days. (Willow has

significantly altered this model in the last few years.) Every weekend
there is a service where people can bring their nonchurched friends.
This service is carefully evaluated on how it will be received or experienced by the nonchurched people attending. Much time, energy
and passion is given to this service by staff and laity. Thus a very
clear message is delivered to everyone that this church cares about
reaching nonchurched people. The idea is to take the most conven-
ient time in the week, Sunday morning, and dedicate it not to
churched people but to the nonchurched. All the people of the church
are then invited to come to a midweek service, known as New Community, where the believers worship together, celebrate what God has
done, learn from God's Word and remind each other of our responsibility to reach the lost.

We bought into this philosophy of how to do church with total
and almost reckless abandon. People began to invite their nonchurched friends. Seekers came to our church and subsequently
brought their own seeker friends. We blanketed the area with postcards advertising the various sermon series we were presenting. As
Willow would describe it in those days, we were seeking to create a
safe place for people to hear a dangerous message. And we were doing
all this in a less than ideal setting. We still weren't able to meet on
Sunday mornings, and we met in a very churchy sanctuary without
theatrical lighting. But we knew this would soon be different.

We were finally able to purchase a piece of undeveloped property
in the middle of town and worked feverishly to remodel twelve modular units (*trailers* is the less gracious term). We created a large-group
meeting space by putting six modular units together, which allowed
us to squeeze in about 350 people at a time. We outfitted this little
catacomb-like auditorium with state-of-the-art sound, lighting and
video. Finally, we could begin to deliver the performance excellence
that we dreamed of. The other modular units became our office space
and children's classrooms. It certainly wasn't Willow-like in its outward appearance, but it was, at least, our own space, and we could
finally meet on Sunday mornings.

We moved into our new location in 1994 and immediately switched our Sunday afternoon service to Thursday night, calling it, predictably, New Community. We moved our Saturday night service to Sunday morning. Our very first Sunday morning we had about four hundred new people attend, and growth just kept climbing after that.

Within a couple of years we had one thousand people coming to Oak Hills, which obviously isn't that many people in the megachurch world, but in our little pond it was impressive. It certainly overwhelmed us. A good number of people who had been attending on Sunday afternoon, but not Saturday night, never quite made the transition with us. It was fine for us to have this seeker service as one of the many things we did as a church, but it was difficult for them when the seeker service became the central focus of the weekend. Still, with hundreds of new people coming, the loss of these old "Oak Hillians" was just part of the price of reaching nonchurched people. We missed them, but we hardly had time to think about it.

I remember being excited and bewildered during those days. In becoming a pastor, I had never thought that much about outward success. I just liked the idea of being a pastor and living in community with people I loved. But this was something I had never anticipated. It was exhilarating and intoxicating. We would finish a service and there would be a long line of people waiting to talk with me. People who wanted to confess sin and who were wondering if God could make a difference in their life. They had just sat through a sixty-five-minute service that was fast-paced, well put together, interesting, compelling, funny, informative, entertaining and emotionally stimulating, and many wanted to see how they could know this God we were talking about.

I remember one such moment with great clarity. I had just finished talking and praying with a long line of people after one of our better conceived and more powerfully performed services, and I went over and plopped down next to our creative arts pastor, Manuel Luz. Manuel was directly responsible for everything that happened in our seeker services and New Community. We knew we had done a very good job that day. From a performance perspective, we had put together a first-rate product. The artistic elements were very compelling and technically excellent. There were times when people were laughing uproariously and others when they were wiping away tears. ("Make them laugh and make them cry"—in some seeker-church circles this is known as the Disney formula.) After settling into the chair next to Manuel, I sighed and said, "Wow!" And with uncharacteristic dark irony Manuel said, "You know, we don't even need God to do this."

Of course both of us knew he was speaking facetiously. Of course we knew that our stated purpose was for building God's kingdom, not our own. And both of us knew that Scripture clearly teaches that without Christ we can do nothing. But we also knew that we had carefully planned that service for exactly the result we had achieved and that we were getting quite good at it. But the fact that I remember this two-minute conversation some fifteen or so years later demonstrates that it conveyed an element of truth. I believe it scared me. But the monster had now been created, and it demanded to be fed.

The decade of the 1990s was a time of great growth and excitement in our church. Our regular weekend attendance hit as high as seventeen hundred people. In our little community that was a pretty impressive thing. It was an invigorating time. New Community was the highlight of every week. Almost four hundred people would come every Thursday night, and we would constantly remind ourselves, as Bill Hybels would say in those days, that the church is the hope of the world. As people were making decisions to become followers of Christ, we felt that we were a part of something very big. Our increasing attendance only served to reinforce the belief that God was up to something and that he was using us to further his work in this world.

In 1997 Mike Lueken joined the staff of Oak Hills. Using the language that was in vogue at that time, he became our pastor of spiritual formation. His job was to give his attention to the back half of our mission statement. Ripping off Willow's well-known mission statement, we were seeking to "turn nonchurched people into a community of fully devoted followers of Christ." Mike was to help all these new people making commitments to Christ to become fully devoted followers of Christ.

During those years we made yearly pilgrimages to Willow for their Church Leadership Conference and the Leadership Summit. We would take dozens of people with us every time. We found that these Willow junkets were the most effective way of infusing new people with the fervor and genius of the Willow model. We believed that we had indeed reoriented our entire church around reaching non-churched people. We had, in many ways, accomplished what we set out to do.

It was also, speaking candidly, a pretty heady time for me person-ally. The rapid growth of our church caused us to be noticed in our area. Somehow Willow found out about us as well. As a result, on several occasions I was invited to meet with a very small group of pas-tors from around the country who had the privilege of spending a few days with Bill Hybels. In a very freewheeling and intimate atmosphere, we listened to him talk about the challenges of leading a large and growing church. This information and training were a tremendous help with the leadership challenges I was facing. In addition, and I say this with some embarrassment, the fact that I was recognized, at least to some degree, as an up-and-coming leader in the seeker-targeted movement filled me with a sense of inflated importance.

IN DEFENSE OF WILLOW CREEK

Since this book is, obviously, a very unapologetic critique of the church in North America today, it is crucial for me to make some clarifying comments about Willow Creek's influence on Oak Hills and on me personally. Since our church's story during the 1990s is intimately tied to the influence of Willow Creek, it may seem that our critique is aimed particularly at Willow. This is simply not true. Our concern is more specifically with the larger church culture in North America, which has a very limited understanding of the gospel of the kingdom of God and an unhealthy focus on outward success. This church culture has reproduced deeply conflicting values in millions of Christians.

We paint here, admittedly, with a very broad stroke. We don't take issue with Willow Creek specifically but with the inherent biblical and formational defects in the broader North American church culture and the large entrepreneurial churches in our country. A pervasive focus in the religious culture throughout North America is that success lies in attracting people, churched and nonchurched, to their particular church organization. This attractional model, we believe, is fundamentally flawed and will not be able to produce in any significant way the kind of Christ followers church leaders want to produce.

The more personal truth for me, though, is that I would not be half the leader I am today without the influence of the ministry of Willow Creek. I cannot think of a church in North America today that has been more influential in challenging churches all across the world to be more intentional in reaching the nonchurched. It is always easy to throw stones at those who are out in front. And Willow has always been out in front.

I have never attended a conference at Willow where I have not been deeply moved and motivated to follow God in more radical and sacrificial ways. Bill Hybels's inspiring and visionary perspective on our life with God and our calling to serve this world with abandon is powerful. In addition, it would be a mistake to understand Willow as representing a stagnant or unchanging view of the church. Willow has always been willing to engage in authentic evaluations of their own ministry. They exhibit a humble introspection and openness to criticism that is developed only among people more committed to the cause of Christ than to their own success. Their recent groundbreaking research on spiritual maturity in their church through the Reveal study is one of many examples of this.

In addition, not only have they stirred up the church in North America to care about nonchurched people, but they have also been at the vanguard of bringing the arts back to the church; they led evangelicals in opening up church leadership to women; they have been a strong voice for the poor, the oppressed and the marginalized in our world, and thus they have been influential in removing the stranglehold of the religious right on evangelicalism. Their very intentional, effective and behind-the-scenes efforts at partnering with ministries dealing with the crisis of HIV/AIDS in Africa has been a marvelous example of what one church can do to make a powerful difference in this world. More recently, their courageous willingness to tackle the thorny and controversial problem of immigration provides much-needed guidance and leadership for the church today.

Because of all this, I find myself deeply conflicted in recounting this aspect of our story. In some ways I feel like a son who owes so much to his father and is truly not as strong as his father, but who is still refusing to take over his father's business because he feels there is something dramatically flawed with it. I fear, at times, that I display a certain disrespect in all this.

FACE-TO-FACE WITH THE MONSTER

Still, as the decade of the 1990s came to a close, there was a creeping sense among many of us in the leadership at Oak Hills that our particular way of doing church had some unavoidable and unhealthy ramifications that were becoming increasingly troublesome. In those days we often used the "monster" metaphor to talk about this.

Mary Shelley's novel *Frankenstein* is a fascinating and hauntingly tragic story of the creation of a monster that is more powerful and more dangerous than its creator ever imagined. Dr. Frankenstein loved this monster, but once created, it soon became clear that Frankenstein would not be able to control it. It had a life of its own.

One of the undeniable truths of the culture of the large entrepreneurial, attractional-model church is that it requires constant feeding. When we structure a church around attracting people to cutting-edge, entertaining, interesting, inspirational and always-growing services and ministries, there is simply no room for letting up. Once we have communicated to the masses that if they come to our church, they'll be surprised, then we have this never-ending burden to surprise people every week. There is no resting. If there is a particularly wonderful experience one weekend, we are driven to do even better the next.

The burden this places on the staff and laity can hardly be overstated. There were times when I felt like I simply did not have it in me to perform again at that level for yet another weekend. Until Mike Lueken came on staff, I was the main speaker at both the seeker services and New Community. It took between twenty-five and thirty hours each week to prepare for those messages. My work week easily and regularly stretched past seventy hours. This was normal life for almost a decade. I knew it was not spiritually healthy for me, but the monster was hungry and needed to be fed. In many ways I had become addicted to the adrenaline rush and the relentless ministry demands of the show. I often found myself stumbling along with a profound sense of depletion. I felt empty. But I am enough of an emotionally repressed Midwesterner that I just took a deep breath and did it again the following week. The cost? My soul was shrinking and my ability to have a clear perspective on what God was up to was severely compromised. It felt as though there was neither the time nor the luxury for deep reflection.

Many in our staff developed a bit of dark humor during this time. While we enjoyed the creative challenge, we were often troubled by the fact that we could never really let up. We would talk about how we could hear the monster beginning to stir again in the fictional basement of our church, and we knew that if we did not feed it, its cage would not hold it. It was too powerful. Therefore, week after week, we all mustered the energy to put on the show one more time.

During these days there was a growing and nagging realization that there simply was no way we could attend carefully to a rich and full life with God and still live at the pace we were living. In addition, we also began to grow increasingly uneasy that this model of doing church might be unhealthy for the people whose understanding of the Christian life was shaped by a church culture that treated them as religious consumers. What would happen if we just stopped performing at this level for a few months? Would they take their business elsewhere? How do we present the radical message of Christ in a church culture that caters to the religious demands of the nominally committed? We might be able to speak on the more radical teachings of Jesus, and we did with some regularity, but our model of doing church was louder. The medium is indeed the message.

These thoughts troubled us whenever we had the space to listen to them. But then we would hear the monster stirring once more, and we would get back to work.

2

DECIDING TO CHANGE

The Donner Party

KENT CARLSON

*D*uring the Christmas season of 1999 we were finally able to move into our first permanent building. It was a massive thirty-seven thousand square-foot facility with an auditorium that would seat twelve hundred people, and it had an immediate and not entirely positive effect on our church. Since 1994 we had been meeting in these modular units with girders at a little over seven feet that kept those of us who were inclined toward raising our hands in worship a bit gun shy about being too exuberant. We could crowbar in about 350 people at a time, and we had been filling this room during our four weekend seeker services and our Thursday night New Community. Now, all of the sudden, we had this cavernous room with a thirty-five-foot ceiling filled with cat-walks, huge twenty-foot screens on either side of the stage, lighting that could create just about any atmosphere we desired, and a sound system designed for up-front performances.

The move from our crowded but intimate auditorium into this massive building was a bit of an adjustment. We were enthralled with the size and all the bells and whistles, but many people experienced a sense of loss. We felt we needed this new building—there simply wasn't enough room for all the new people who were coming—but the contrast was so extreme that it left many of us with conflicting feelings. But the weekends kept coming with an oppressive regularity, which didn't leave us with room for too much navel-gazing.

With a huge building and budget it was necessary for us to keep growing, and we did, but not quite as quickly as we anticipated. We had planned for about a 50 percent growth rate, but our actual growth was more like 20 percent. This still increased our weekend attendance to over seventeen hundred people, but we were not satisfied with this. We immersed ourselves in all the various church-growth strategies and kept analyzing how we could continue to attract new people and fold them into the life and ministry of the church.

As we moved into the summer of 2000, and in preparation for a leadership retreat we were planning in July at Donner Lake, California (unwittingly choosing the location of the infamous wagon-train disaster of 1846-1847), I had everyone who was invited read *The Very Large Church* by Lyle Schaller. We knew that in order to grow at the pace we intended, we would have to keep learning new skills and continue to restructure our staff in order to accommodate this growth. It seemed like the perfect book to help us do this. Its impact on us, though, was not what I intended (but I'll get into that in a moment).

STRUGGLING WITH CONFLICTING VALUES

It would be inaccurate and grossly unfair to characterize ourselves during these days as completely and blindly obsessed with outward success and numerical growth. The true story is much more complicated than that. As I have mentioned, in the midst of the outward success we were experiencing, we had a troubling sense that all the external activity was not entirely beneficial for our spiritual formation. When we had the space in our lives to attend to this, we found ourselves hungering for a life with God that had more substance, more depth, more reality.

In our pursuit of this, many of us in leadership in the church were reading authors who were on the opposite end of the spectrum from all the church-growth training we were receiving. We read contemporary Catholic authors such as Thomas Merton and Henri Nouwen. Richard Foster and Eugene Peterson are examples of other contemporary authors who introduced us to a world that was dramatically different from the church-growth culture we were immersed in. We were drawn to the writings of those who seemed to understand this deeper life with God with greater clarity. It was not uncommon for us to be reading the desert fathers, Bernard of Clairvaux, St. John of the Cross and Teresa of Ávila at the same time we were developing a strategic plan to help us grow to three thousand people and learning how to build an effective small-group structure that would keep people from leaving through the back door.

Eventually we got our hands on some of the books and articles being written by Dallas Willard, a professor of philosophy at the University of Southern California. His writings began to infect our minds with so many thought viruses that we found ourselves in an almost constant state of ecclesiastical disequilibrium. In his gentle and biblically rigorous way, Willard argued that spiritual growth into the image of Christ is to be the normal experience of the follower of Christ. To follow Christ in any meaningful sense requires that we must be profoundly transformed. We spoke endlessly about this and struggled with the obvious truth that this kind of transformation was not the normative experience of the average follower of Christ. Even more troubling, we realized that it was not even our own experience.

It was a somewhat odd and conflicting season in the church. On the one hand we were vigorously engaged in and at times overwhelmed by the never-ending demands of growing a large church, while on the other we found ourselves profoundly drawn to a different pace of life and ministry that invited us to drink deeply from the limitless grace and goodness of God. We did not know it at the time but these conflicting influences in our lives would not coexist easily. Indeed, they cannot coexist peacefully, for they are built on completely different foundational understandings of the life God has invited us to live. The stage was being set for a rather tumultuous experience.

Shortly before our senior staff and lay leadership retreat at Donner Lake, Mike Lueken enrolled in a two-week Doctor of Ministry class led by Dallas Willard, which proved to be one of the watershed events in the life of Oak Hills. Mike came back from this class thoroughly unsettled by the vision of life in the kingdom of God that Willard so convincingly presents. The contrast between the transformative power of this kingdom life and the high-pressure, frenetic, crazy-paced life of the entrepreneurial, attractional model church can hardly be overstated. Mike, I and a few others were engaged in constant conversations about what this might mean.

ENCOUNTERING GOD AT DONNER LAKE

All this brings us back to our July leadership retreat and the reading of *The Very Large Church*. The book, like most of Schaller's books, is well-researched and heavily pragmatic. Schaller doesn't spend a lot of time probing the theological, biblical or formational implications of growing a very large church. He just explores how to do it. And there was one chapter in this book that affected almost every single one of us who read it in preparation for our retreat. The chapter is titled "The Consequences of Consumerism." For some reason this chapter bothered us. Schaller was trying to honestly deal with the very real issue of consumerism as a powerful force in North American life, and by extension its influence in the subculture of North American Christianity. After presenting the various challenges of consumerism, he made this very straightforward and unsettling comment:

> The big issue, however, is not whether one applauds or disapproves of the growth of consumerism. The central issue is that consumerism is now a fact of life, and this raises the question of how your congregation will respond to this change in the societal context. The consequences of consumerism are real, and they have radically transformed the context for the

parish ministry. Do you identify this new context as a source of despair? Or as a challenge to your creativity?

As we gathered together at Donner Lake in July of 2000 and began to discuss Schaller's book, this chapter was immediately brought up as a topic of conversation. It seemed that the message of the chapter is that consumerism is a powerful force in North American culture, perhaps the most powerful, and there is nothing anyone can do to stop it. Since it is an unavoidable fact of life, church leaders should determine how they will harness this force rather than railing against it uselessly.

Schaller didn't say it with such stark and glaring words, but that is how we received it. To a person, it deeply bothered us. As we wrestled with these issues and voiced our almost visceral reaction to the veiled suggestion that it might be best to simply resign ourselves to the necessity of exploiting consumerism, something very real and extremely unexpected happened among us. God met us in the space of a few hours in a powerful and life-changing and church-changing way.

To put all this in context I should explain that our church does not have a history of hearing from God in dramatic fashion, which results in some drastic reshaping of our mission. I am not making a value judgment about churches or Christian leaders who have such encounters with God as a regular occurrence. Of course, there are undoubtedly inherent difficulties and dangers with that style of ministry, but that is not my point in mentioning this. I only mention this to point out that our church, and myself personally, are probably on the other end of the spectrum. We tend to lean toward strategic and pragmatic planning, not detailed instructions from God as to what we should be doing next. Obviously, this bias for trusting human strategy and planning carries with it, perhaps, an even greater degree of difficulty and danger. I merely bring all this up to point out that when God met us at this retreat, and as a result, our church was drastically changed; it was a very unusual and unexpected experience for us.

Those who were at this retreat have their own personal memories of what took place in those next few hours. We all remember that Schaller's chapter about consumerism was the catalyst for much of the discussion. In retrospect, perhaps it was this issue of consumerism that brought the conflicting values of external success and authentic spiritual formation into such sharp contrast. Gradually, we began to get some clarity on a troubling truth: attracting people to church based on their consumer demands is in direct and irredeemable conflict with inviting people, in Jesus' words, to lose their lives in order to find them. It slowly began to dawn on us that our method of attracting people was forming them in ways contrary to the way of Christ.

It was not so much that we were engaging in a bait-and-switch approach to ministry, although that might indeed have been the case. The real issue, we believed, was far more insidious than that. We began to realize that our current church structure was actually working against the invitation of Christ to experience his authentic transformation. In order to help people follow Christ more fully, we would have to work against the very methods we were using to attract people to our church. As person after person shared at this retreat, we slowly began to realize that, to be faithful to the gospel of Jesus, consumerism was not a force to be harnessed but rather an antibiblical value system that had to be prophetically challenged.

Somewhere during this discussion, I remember sharing, with a kind of stream of consciousness, how much I had been motivated in the last few years by my own personal ambition. I liked the feeling of being the senior pastor of a large and successful church. I just blurted it aloud. As I said it, I remember having a distinct sense, not of a stern rebuke from God, but rather a gentle, "OK, but that's enough of that now. Let us go on to better things."

Somewhere in the midst of all this there were a few minutes of complete silence. Everyone had finished what they needed to say and we all sat in the silence, realizing that something very powerful was happening. One of our lay leaders, a dear friend who has been with the church from the very beginning, finally broke the silence with these simple words, "This is a holy moment." Someone else suggested that we should pray. And we did.

Over the next day or two we tried to summarize what we felt we were hearing from God. It seemed to us that we were being called to invite people to have authentic encounters with Jesus that would result in transformation and a contagious expression of our faith. One person wryly commented that sixteen years into the history of Oak Hills we were finally deciding to center our church around Jesus. Not exactly radical stuff. But it seemed radical to us.

There was a pervasive sense among all of us that to be faithful to what had occurred at Donner Lake, our church would have to change rather dramatically. We were not being called to a gentle tweaking of some church programs. This was going to be a major overhaul.

There was, though, an amazing sense of unity and resolve among the leaders at this retreat. Together, we all had this experience with God. There was no denying it. We knew we had to be faithful to follow through with what God had done among us. This sense of unity and resolve proved to be crucially important in the very turbulent years that followed.

As we left the retreat and headed back to the challenge of implementing this change of focus at our church, we acknowledged that this adventure might come at some cost. This was an amazing understatement. The truth is, we had no idea what we were getting into.

3

THE KEYS TO TRANSITION

A Few Hard Years

MIKE LUEKEN

*O*ver the years we've had some of our best leadership meetings when we aren't formally meeting. We call them "deck conversations." We are relaxing on a backyard deck and a clarifying discussion breaks out. Sometimes profound conversations happen on the deck that open our eyes, crystallize our thoughts or focus our direction.

During one of these deck gatherings during our Donner retreat, an elder said that if we were to take seriously the call to help people "seek first the kingdom of God" (Matthew 6:33 ESV) our church would radically change. We all knew he was right, but we had no idea what it would actually entail. It's probably better that we didn't, because had we known, we may have found a way to dismiss the whole ordeal and forge ahead, business as usual.

We returned from Donner knowing, at least at some level, that what happened there was a seminal event in the history of our church. In one sense, over its twenty-five year existence, the focus of Oak Hills has remained fairly consistent. The early years were about building a loving community of people who were seeking God together. The seeker season was an entire decade of vision casting and building programs to reach nonchurched people. We were embroiled in the work of vision casting, planning and designing strategies to fulfill this compelling mission.

But in another sense, we have a taste for the new and innovative. Our staff cringes whenever Kent and I go on a retreat because there is a good chance we will return with a new idea. We both lean toward conceptual, theological thinking. We enjoy experimenting with creative ideas and imagining new ministries and strategies. These new ideas often mean a staff person will have another helping of responsibility added to their already-full plate. At times our staff gets whiplash trying to follow our latest interest. So they weren't surprised when we returned from our Donner retreat animated by what had occurred. They had seen us this way many times.

The days and weeks after Donner became a running conversation with our staff; we were trying to bring them up to speed on what had happened. It was difficult to re-create the experience. We were like small children who can recognize people's faces and point to objects but haven't the vocabulary or ability to articulate. We were learning a new language. We vigorously resist the "God spoke to us" card because it can overpower the opposition and end conversations. But we felt God had spoken to us. We were processing what we thought he said while trying to explain it to staff at the same time. Kent and I spent significant time together trying to find words for the experience. We had countless meetings with staff, elders and others in the church. We talked about the possible ramifications. It took several months, but the staff gradually realized this was not a retreat "high." We weren't recovering. Something had happened in the mountains.

JUST TELL ME WHAT TO DO!

Those initial experiences of trying to explain the implications of the Donner retreat to our staff were a foreshadowing of perhaps the biggest challenge we've faced in the ten years of this adventure. People wanted to know the practical implications. They wanted to know what they needed to do to put the emphasis on spiritual formation into action. I recently received a phone call from a person who heard about our church at a conference. They were calling to find out how our church was different now that we were stressing spiritual formation. They were asking the practical, programmatic question.

But the story of Oak Hills is not only in the specific, practical changes that we made to our services and programs. We eventually made many, and we continue to work to provide realistic means that help people be formed into Christ. But the first order of business after the Donner retreat was to reshape the theological and conceptual foundation of our church. The first practical thing to do was to jackhammer the foundation on which we had built our church. There was no way to avoid this if we were going to make the radical cultural shift we felt God was calling us to at Donner. We went back to the basics and essentially started over. We did it in our teaching. We did it in conversations with our staff. We did it on the elder board. And we did it in the various meetings we had with individuals and ministry teams. We asked basic questions all over again. What is the good news? What are we called to do in response to it? What is the purpose of the church? How does the church relate to a consumer-driven culture? To understand the story of Oak Hills is to understand that we spent several years sorting through these kinds of questions. A frustrating fog of vagueness hovered over our church for many years. People were antsy to know what they were supposed to do. They wanted programs to enroll in, classes to attend and strategies to implement. But new programs would never bring about the radical cultural shift. We needed a new foundation.

Eugene Peterson captures the essence of the issue:

If Christ is King, everything, quite literally, every *thing* and every *one,* has to be re-imagined, re-configured, re-oriented to a way of life that consists in an obedient following of Jesus. This is not easy. It is not accomplished by participating in a prayer

meeting or two, or signing up for a seven-step course in discipleship at school or church, or attending an annual prayer
breakfast. A total renovation of our imagination, our way of
looking at things—what Jesus commanded in his no-nonsense
imperative, "Repent!"—is required.

We have spent the majority of our time the last ten years attempting
to "renovate the imaginations" of our people.

IT STARTS WITH US

While we did not know the practical implications of the Donner retreat for Oak Hills, intuitively we knew the radical change had to
begin with us. It had to begin in our own hearts with our own transformation. We could not merely talk about the transformation God
could bring. We had to experience it. The transition had to begin with
those of us in leadership engaging in the processes and practices that
would inspire spiritual growth. Donner was not about a new paradigm or strategy for growing the church. It wasn't a program change.
We weren't replacing the seeker-targeted model with a spiritual formation strategy. Something divine and profound happened to us at
Donner. We had finally heard the gospel. It was fresh. It was real. It
was attractive. And we knew we could not separate ourselves from the
message. If spiritual formation was going to be established as the driving force at Oak Hills, it had to first take root in our own hearts.

The outward success of our church came with a steep price tag.
We had grown the church, but we were not more like Jesus. Growing
the church did not require that we be like Jesus. It wasn't as though
we were blatantly sinning and trying to hide it. But the leadership
energy required in a larger church and the adrenaline rush of outward success gradually substituted for authentic experiences with
God. The enthusiastic buzz in the church validated what we were
doing. The hard work of preparing insightful sermons replaced hearing God's voice in his Word. We had built a thriving church, but we
were not becoming better people in whom Christ was being formed.
Perhaps in some ways we knew this was happening while it was hap-

pening. But the cause was too crucial to let anything get in its way. We had to keep cranking out a quality product. Under the rallying cry of "lost people matter to God," our soul viruses went unchecked.

Post-Donner, we had to do ministry differently. Who we were and who we were becoming was more important than a successful church. We could not lead our church into a program of formation. It was time to face ourselves. It was time to deal with our duplicity, the ugliness of our motivations, the size of our egos and our runaway ambition.

We needed unhurried, luxurious time in solitude, doing nothing. We needed to experiment with simplicity. We needed to deal with our anger and lust. We needed to learn how to abandon the outcome of our work. We needed to slow down. We needed to learn how to be with God without an agenda. Obviously we couldn't put the church on hold while we focused on our own formation. But Donner was an experience with God that awoke us from a complacency that had been cultivated over many years of vocational ministry. We had to rigorously pursue our own formation. From the beginning, the transition at Oak Hills had to begin with God doing something real in our hearts.

GOING PUBLIC

In the fall of 2000 we did a sermon series titled "Genuine Experiences with Jesus" at our midweek worship service. This was our first attempt to tell the church what had occurred at our summer retreat. This series was one of the first steps in the long, grinding process of changing the Oak Hills culture. Throughout the series we stressed the importance of having real encounters with God. We talked about church being a place where we meet Jesus and become more like him. We made our first attempts to push against the performance orientation of our seeker services. It was strange to make a big deal about having real, life-changing encounters with Jesus. Did we need a retreat and a word from God to learn this? We took a stab at explaining the meaning of the kingdom of God. We cast a vision of the life God has for us in his kingdom. We taught on the importance of intention in the spiritual formation journey. We unpacked a few of the foundational spiritual disciplines. These things were not entirely new to our congregation. But the urgency with which we talked about them was. We invited different elders to share their perspectives on the retreat.

This series marked the beginning of a new chapter in our church's history. The few weeks we spent teaching these things did not radically change our church. We didn't expect it would. But the conversation was beginning to change.

CHANGING THE SEEKER SERVICE

We realized that our weekend service had to change to better reflect who we wanted to be. The weekend services embodied and conveyed the vision and values of the church. So to be a church oriented around spiritual formation, we had to incorporate this into the weekend services.

For ten years we had been holding a typical seeker service. It was approximately sixty-five minutes long with minimal participation required by the congregation. We sang a worship chorus or two. There was a drama, a few performance songs and a message.

Gradually, we changed the weekend experience. We lengthened it by fifteen minutes. We spent the additional time in worship. The preaching centered on the kingdom of God. We constantly talked about transformation. We waded into the details of anger, lust, worry, fear and control, and constantly tried to help people imagine their lives without these things. We stressed the importance of spending time with God in solitude and silence. We encouraged people to go away by themselves and do nothing.

The weekend services were beginning to orient around the importance of the kingdom of God and spiritual transformation.

CANCELING NEW COMMUNITY

In time, the weekend service began to resemble New Community. New Community was the weekly event where "Oak Hillians" gathered for worship, nurture and community. Over the years as our seeker service attendance had grown, so had the priority we placed on New Community. It was easy to remain anonymous at the weekend service. New Community was often the starting point for a deeper connection with God and others. We constantly invited the weekend crowd to attend the Thursday service. Our motto was, "If you want to know Oak Hills, you have to come to New Community." We challenged people to make Thursday night a priority in their schedule. By the summer of 2000 the attendance was around 350. Over the years this midweek worship service had become a crucial component of our ministry. Many felt New Community was one of the best things happening at Oak Hills.

But now we were doing virtually the same thing on Thursday and Sunday. Around this time we began thinking more carefully about what people actually need in order to grow deeper in Christ. If a churchgoing Christ follower asked for guidance on how to move toward maturity, we would probably not suggest they attend another worship service. We would encourage them to spend time in silence and solitude, memorize Scripture or walk into the scars from their past. We would invite them to become part of a small group where Christ-centered community happens. We might suggest they find a place to serve other people.

As our two weekly services starting losing their distinctiveness, we began considering eliminating New Community. After many long conversations in various leadership settings, in the autumn of 2001 we made the hard decision to cancel our midweek New Community service.

In the latter part of 2001 we announced the decision to the church. The last service was scheduled for the middle of March 2002. Thereafter New Community would happen once a month. This was perhaps the most significant visible change of our ten-year journey. New Community had been a staple of our ministry for a long time. Canceling it took away a life-giving component to the people of our church.

In truth, we were moving New Community to the weekends and eliminating the seeker service. But people didn't see it this way. They

saw that the seeker service had already changed; it wasn't the show it
had once been. Now we were getting rid of the midweek service. People
felt we were taking away the top two things happening at the church.
They were right. Canceling New Community made a loud statement
about our intention to reorient the church around spiritual formation.

People immediately reacted. We received a number of e-mails asking for clarification. Many thought we had lost our minds. We had
special forums where the congregation could ask questions and raise
concerns. After working at it for several months, people seemed to
slowly accept the decision. They accepted it, that is, until the service
was actually canceled. In late March 2002, there was no longer a New
Community service to attend. When that occurred, and for years
after, the decision to cancel the service became more real and painful
for many.

When we tell our kids in September there won't be many Christmas presents this year because we are flying to Grandma's house,
they nod in agreement and assure us they understand. But on December 25 when they are staring at a tree with nothing under it, reality
hits them. They start asking questions. They wonder why there aren't
any gifts.

Perhaps the words alone strike our intellect while the actual
change drives into our heart. Whatever the cause, for years people
expressed their disappointment in our decision to eliminate the midweek worship service. I think it is accurate to say that we under-
estimated the unifying dynamic of this service. It bonded our church
together. There was a unique experience at New Community that
could not be duplicated at the weekend services. It happened at night.
It was the middle of the week. It was a smaller group. People knew
each other. They could look across the room and see dozens of people
they knew and had worshiped and served with for years. The congregation was severely affected by canceling this service.

We began having New Community once a month as planned, but
almost immediately the attendance declined dramatically. The once-
a-month experiment only lasted a year. Looking back it's as though a

dam broke on the heels of the New Community decision. We heard stinging criticisms. People wrote e-mails, called and made appointments. There was a growing heaviness in the air. The church was losing its groove. Some people were concerned that Kent and I had lost our way. Staff and elder meetings were dominated by conversations about managing the damage. The Donner retreat had ultimately led to the New Community decision. Now the dominoes started falling. Growing numbers of people were displeased. And many began voting on the decision by leaving the church.

In December 2001 our attendance at our three weekend services was around seventeen hundred, including children. But this number was dropping at an alarming rate. Every few months we were losing more people, and not only fringe people. We were hearing stories about longtime Oak Hillians who had decided to leave. While we expected a certain amount of fallout from the changes we were making, we never anticipated the attendance decline we actually experienced. We estimate that since the end of 2001 we have had a net loss of approximately one thousand people. Today we average around 750 at our two Sunday services.

THE IMPACT ON THE STAFF

With attendance declining, we were facing mounting financial pressure. At the time of the Donner retreat, we were staffed to be a church of two thousand or more. For example, in the worship/arts area, we had four full-time and one part-time staff to cover our two services (weekend and New Community). With the canceling of New Community, declining attendance and shrinking offerings, we needed to reduce staff in this area. In addition, our children's ministry had two full-time and three part-time staff, and cuts would have to be made there as well. The layoffs happened over the span of several years. Ministry expenses were sliced to bare bones. In addition, more than once we instituted staff-wide pay cuts. Our elders matched our sacrifice by increasing their giving by the amount of our pay cuts. Overall since 2000, we've reduced our staff by ten people. Financially, it has helped to have fewer salaries to pay. But especially in the early years of the transition, the church was already losing momentum, and the reduction of staff added to the prevailing opinion that we were in trouble and perhaps had lost our way.

The question of staffing went beyond financial constraints. The more we transitioned, the more we realized that in some cases we did not have the right people on staff. The seeker style was program driven. The service was a well-crafted performance designed to keep people interested so they would continue to come. We wanted staff that were high-energy, competent leaders, who could crank out a quality product and assimilate people into their programs. We hired staff to build new leaders who could take over their ministry. We evaluated our staff almost exclusively on numerically based growth.

When we returned from Donner we were speaking the new language of spiritual formation. We prioritized who we were becoming, slowing down and spending time in solitude. Some staff quickly recognized the tectonic shift that was happening at Oak Hills. Others were well-trained in the seeker model and did not know how to process what we were saying. They had been expected to produce, and they did. Ironically, though they were technically pastors, we had not really asked them to nurture people in becoming more like Jesus. They had not been trained to help someone walk into the details of their own heart and soul and cooperate with the Holy Spirit to become more like Christ. They had become proficient at performing and producing. Some of these staff struggled to understand why we were abandoning the proven seeker strategy. They weren't tracking with our mounting concerns about consumerism. The experience we had at Donner did not resonate with them. We worked at trying to help them process what was happening. But eventually it became clear that some who had helped us succeed as a seeker church were not able to make the transition to the spiritual formation emphasis.

In 2002 one of our key pastors resigned. It was a complex, difficult process. But over a period of many months and hard conversations, we mutually agreed it was the best thing to do. This man loved the church and had served it well, and the congregation loved him. His departure came at a fragile time. People were already on edge about what was happening, and this added to their concern about the stability of our leadership. Not long after, another staff person resigned for moral reasons. This crisis took months to sort through and likewise added to the angst and concern people felt about the church.

At one point in the midst of all this we asked one of our elders to join us for a staff meeting. Kent and I were informing the staff of our intention to become co–senior pastors, and we wanted the input and support of this long-tenured elder. When the meeting ended, he simply told us we had lost our staff. He could feel it in the room. He could see it in some of their eyes. There was a lack of community. The years spent growing the church left little time for staff relationships. Now we were making wholesale changes. Things were happening fast and furious. The staff was caught in the middle. We got along fine, but we were not a unified, close community.

At our annual staff retreat that year, we broke into two groups. Kent was with one and I with the other. We invited them to share their frustrations, concerns and questions. After about two hours, the groups switched. It was not easy to listen to their critiques. But our staff let us know they wanted more than job assignments and vision casting. They were united in their desire for deeper community.

After this retreat we began meeting together every Tuesday for lunch and study. Over the past several years this weekly hour and a half together has significantly increased our community with one another. We have read several books together. We laugh together. We spend time praying through various needs in the church. Our purposefulness in building these relationships has helped us navigate the many storms we faced these past ten years.

LOOKING FOR MODELS
Shortly after we began making the changes previously described, we began looking for other leaders and churches who had made a similar transition. However, it was not easy to find help. Fortunately, we had

a few people in our church who were ahead of us in terms of their understanding of spiritual formation because of their own study and learning on the topic. They had a desire for formation to be more central at Oak Hills and gently encouraged us to follow the path of figuring out how to make this work at our church.

A series of events and relationships allowed us to host a Renovaré regional conference at Oak Hills in the spring of 2001. Richard Foster and Dallas Willard came and taught about the kingdom of God to the hundreds who had gathered from around our area. Hosting this conference was another component in the protracted process of changing our church culture. It helped drive the stake further into the ground. For years we had actively recruited people to join us at Willow Creek's annual Church Leadership Conference. The Renovaré conference prioritized an entirely different set of concerns. The fact that we were hosting this event reinforced the transition we were making.

It also helped reinforce the message of the kingdom we had begun to proclaim. We were able to make connections with other people who were outside our church but were enthusiastic about what was happening at Oak Hills. The conference helped us realize there are pockets of people in every congregation who are hungry for the gospel of the kingdom and the new life it brings. This was another confirmation that we were on the right road, even though at times the journey was difficult.

THE ROLE OF THE ELDER BOARD

The early years of our transition may sound exceedingly negative. They *were* long years. Many times we wondered if we had missed a turn. Our elder board meetings were consumed with navigating one crisis or another related to the transition. One week it was the decreasing attendance. The next it was our tight finances. The next it was a bubble of discontent surfacing in one subgroup or another within the congregation. These meetings often ended with a gut check on the direction we had chosen. Was God in it? Did we still believe he had spoken to us? Should we keep going in spite of the challenges we were facing? Each time there was a hint of doubt about the direction we had chosen, an elder renewed our resolve by expressing that we were irrevocably committed to this process. Without question the various women and men who have served on our elder board over the past decade are the heroes of this transition.

It seems there are two routes a church can take in attempting to orient more fully around the gospel of the kingdom and spiritual formation. First, hungry individuals and small groups scattered throughout a congregation can pursue this new way of living on their own. As they do this in the shadows, the leadership waits for it to slowly and subversively infiltrate the culture of the church. Over time, hopefully, the infection spreads and the DNA of the church gradually changes.

The second route is a more centralized pursuit of the kingdom life with a corresponding overhaul of the church's structures and strategies to support this pursuit. Every ministry, staff, program and initiative is evaluated on the basis of whether or not it helps people become apprentices of Jesus. This is the route we chose at Oak Hills.

Like many larger churches, the culture of Oak Hills encourages staff to provide strong and skillful leadership to their ministries while building teams of volunteers. We don't operate as a democracy. Staff leads and the elder board protects. One of the biggest questions we faced through this transition was how to bring a congregation of hundreds of people at varying levels of commitment and interest along with us. The Donner experience happened to a group of ten leaders. It's taken years to infiltrate the lifeblood of the church with an emphasis on spiritual formation. The elder board has been crucial in this process. Kent and I are fairly strong leaders, but we could never force-feed a shift this dramatic down the throats of our elders, staff or congregation. From the beginning our elder board willingly embraced this transition with unwavering confidence in God's leadership. They linked their arms with ours and have never once broke ranks.

There have been countless deck conversations to process the adventure. We have spent hours together dreaming of what our church could be as a catalyst for spiritual formation in the lives of our people. They have fully engaged with the many problems and issues that have emerged over the years. Kent and I have never once felt like we were on our own, navigating this ecclesiastical quagmire by ourselves. Our elder board has been on the adventure with us.

Shortly after we returned from the Donner experience, both Kent and I experienced intense personal difficulty. At times, the pressure of leading through this change, coupled with these personal challenges, kept us from operating at full strength. Our elder board always came alongside and encouraged. They kept believing in us even when we were not functioning at full capacity. They never hesitated to give us time to tease out our tension. They were extraordinarily mature in their ability to see the big picture. In the early years of the transition, many of our long-held beliefs and practices were being dislodged. As a result, both Kent and I spent long seasons drowning in angst and unanswerable questions about the church and its role in the world. The elders were unbelievably patient with the bumps we hit along the way.

Like us, the elder board received many complaints and criticisms about what was happening at Oak Hills. They were diligent in communicating their own struggles, but never broke ranks.

At one point early in the transition, Kent and I received an especially difficult e-mail from a group of lay leaders within one of our ministries. They took off the gloves and smacked us about as hard as they could. They even suggested that Satan had broadsided us. Our elder board decided this needed to be confronted face to face. Two of the elders met with this group of people and skillfully challenged the wisdom of writing such a missive. A very seasoned elder read the letter aloud, after which he peered over the top of his reading glasses and simply asked them if they all agreed with what the letter said. The room was quiet. So he read it again and asked the same question. It was an exquisite display of assertive spiritual leadership.

Though there were many setbacks throughout the course of our transition, the elder board never lost its resolve to follow this path. In the midst of falling attendance and offerings, they kept the big picture in mind and stayed the course. They didn't sweat the little things. In those times when Kent and I were reeling, they carried the vision and offered encouragement.

Their extraordinary leadership was costly. They carried a burden of leadership that few people in our church will ever realize. They were carrying a vision, trying to hold a congregation together and often trying to manage the volatile interior lives of two struggling senior pastors. The elders paid a price for this in their own soul and relationships.

We've shared our story in enough settings to know how unusual it is to have an elder board like the one we have. But a transition like the one at Oak Hills requires a committed group of mature elders who can lead through turmoil. It would have been impossible to make this transition without this astonishing group of men and women. Their faithful leadership in our lives and in the life of the church has been a sterling testimony to how God works through people to bring about his good purposes. It's been a privilege for us to be surrounded by such uncommon commitment and loyalty.

4

RETHINKING THE GOSPEL

The Enthralling Vision of
Life in God's Kingdom

MIKE LUEKEN

I was converted in the summer of 2000.

That summer I attended a Fuller Seminary class taught by Dallas Willard at a convent in San Francisco. Spirituality and Ministry had been recommended to me by a couple of friends who had taken the course a few years earlier. I had read Dr. Willard's *The Divine Conspiracy*, and was fascinated with his description of the gospel of the kingdom.

From the moment class began, I started to unravel. Over the next two weeks God began to overhaul my understanding of the gospel. Near the end of one of our sessions, Dallas was reflecting on the wonder of the good news. He spoke of the joy, power and possibility of transformation available to those who will trust Christ in all things. I was on the edge of my seat, listening hard, trying to not miss a word. I desperately hoped he was telling the truth. God's good reign and gracious rule was open to all who hungered for life the way it was intended. The Beatitudes were written to hopeless people for whom Christ offered a new and eternal kind of life that could begin now and never end. By placing our confidence in Jesus, we could experience power from God, real joy, forgiveness of sins, peace with God, victory over sin and, if that wasn't enough, an eternity with God. I felt I was hearing this stunningly good news for the first time.

I'd been in church most of my life, attended a rigorous, Bible-centered seminary and preached many sermons on the good news. I had been engrossed in seeker ministry for several years where regular invitations to trust Christ were given. But the years of sitting in church, serving as a pastor and ignoring my own heart perforated my faith in God and joy in the gospel. Willard's class awakened me from a spiritual coma induced by overfamiliarity and disappointment.

I was disappointed with the grind of pastoral ministry. I was disappointed with the stubborn blemishes on the bride of Christ. I was disappointed with the wide gap between what I claimed to believe and who I actually was when I was off stage and behind closed doors. I was disappointed with my anger. I was disappointed by "mature" Christians who acted like spoiled children. I was disappointed with the dog-and-pony show of large church ministry. I was tired of catering to Christians who loved their weekly church fix but continued to orient their lives around their wants, needs and desires. These tensions raced through me with varying degrees of intensity as I listened to Dr. Willard. Like many who have taken this class, it was a watershed in my faith journey.

When I returned to work, every meeting became an excuse to share what I had learned. I had no idea what I was talking about, but I couldn't stop talking about it. It would have been enough if this was a gift from God for my personal enrichment. But my experience was one chapter of a larger story God was writing at our church. It was only a month or so after the class in San Francisco that our leadership team had the previously described Donner experience (see chap. 2), which started Oak Hills on this fascinating journey.

EVERYTHING TURNS ON THE GOSPEL

At its essence the Donner experience was the beginning of a long exercise in rethinking our understanding of the gospel. A combination of factors coalesced to inspire this fresh look at the good news. Our own disillusionment with the megachurch was one factor. We had a growing sense that there had to be more to our ministry than providing thrilling weekend services that steadily increased attendance. Another factor was our resistance to feeding the epidemic of religious consumerism. In addition, Dallas Willard's writings and teachings gave us a fresh vision of life under God and sparked a latent longing in our souls. We began to imagine church in a different way. The Holy Spirit used all of these things to help us reimagine the scope and core message of the gospel.

Occasionally we are asked to explain the primary difference between Oak Hills today and our seeker days. The simple answer is the difference in how we understand the gospel. People are usually dissatisfied with the vagueness of this response. They want harder evidence. They want to know the practical things we did to shift the orientation of our church. But the nexus of our change was a refurbished gospel. Everything that has happened at Oak Hills began by carefully reconsidering the essence of the good news.

THE WONDER OF THE KINGDOM

For many, rethinking the gospel evokes images of a dreary process. It is hardly something we can do with any hope of actually discovering anything new or inspirational. We didn't set out to do this. The Donner experience reopened our hearts to the possibility that the gospel was bigger than we had made it. But this was a gracious work of God's Spirit.

We were quickly enchanted with the idea that the kingdom of God had come in the person of Jesus. "'The time has come,' [Jesus] said. 'The kingdom of God has come near. Repent and believe the good news!'" (Mark 1:15). The good news is that the reign of God over all of life is now available in Jesus Christ. His reign and rule can now be a reality in our lives, as it is in heaven. His love, joy, peace, patience, courage and grace is now available to those who will trust him as their King.

The Great Commission says, "Therefore go and make disciples of all nations, baptizing them in the name of the Father and of the Son and of the Holy Spirit, and teaching them to obey everything I have commanded you. And surely I am with you always, to the very end of the age" (Matthew 28:19-20). The clear call is to make disciples of Jesus who are immersed in a new, trinitarian reality. Disciples are students. They are apprentices of a skillful master.

We were enthralled with the idea of the gospel as an invitation to be an apprentice of Jesus. "Take my yoke upon you and learn from me, for I am gentle and humble in heart, and you will find rest for your souls. For my yoke is easy and my burden is light" (Matthew 11:29-30). Apprentices are learning from Jesus how to live in the kingdom of God, and to trust him with everything, not just their sin problem. They are learning how to experience the life they long for and are made for, under God's gracious, loving and good reign and rule. Apprentices are learning to turn away from self and bring their kingdom into God's kingdom. They are learning to let him have say over their lives. As they restructure their lives around him, he gradually transforms their inner being in Christlikeness. They actually become more like him. They don't obey him because they have to or are trying hard; obedience flows out of the new heart God has fashioned within them.

This renewed understanding of the gospel brings a new view of what it means to be a Christian. A Christian is learning to trust Jesus in everything. By grace, Christians follow his example and teaching. They apply themselves to the various practices, experiences and relationships that help them learn how to do what Jesus said. By God's grace they gradually become the kind of people who naturally and easily obey him. They constantly revise their life to carry through on their decision to follow Jesus. It is an all-encompassing way of living where daily events, circumstances, character challenges and relationships are brought under the gracious and good reign of Jesus Christ. We found renewed passion in the idea of becoming a church that actually helped people live this way.

We began to realize the gospel is bigger and grander than a private transaction between a sinner and God. It encompasses more than we had preached. It is reconciliation at the deepest of levels. It is shalom, the flourishing of all of life. The more we considered the implications of the gospel, the more we became enchanted and enthralled. The news was once again exquisitely good. And it was radically different than the gospel we had been proclaiming.

THE MEANS IS THE MESSAGE

As a seeker church we had regular sermon series on subjects like family, marriage and personal finances. We used blockbuster movie titles as a springboard into relevant topics. Our series raised questions like "What would Jesus say to Lady Gaga?" in the hopes of arousing seekers' interest. These series were intended to teach the Bible but were also designed to keep people pouring into our building. At the end of these teaching series we invited people to become followers of Christ.

From the beginning of our seeker experience, we had ministries and programs available to help people grow in their faith. We had classes for new Christians. We strongly encouraged involvement in small groups and attendance at New Community. We challenged people to find a place to use their gifts in service. We never intentionally truncated the gospel. But our words are only one factor that shapes the message people actually hear.

The way we did church, the style of our services, the underlying values behind our ministry—these communicated a "gospel" in which accepting Jesus was required but apprenticeship to him was optional. It didn't matter what our mission statement said about turning nonchurched people into fully devoted followers of Christ. Discipleship was a department in the church, but not a central tenet of the gospel we proclaimed. So while we had ministries geared toward discipleship, the heart of the church was to attract more people and help them make decisions for Christ. Once they did, we hoped they would assimilate into the life of our church. Our time and energy was spent dealing with the ongoing maintenance of a growing church machine. On our way to becoming a successful suburban church, we had abridged the gospel.

There is a familiar axiom that says, "The message never changes, but the methods always change." The idea is that our communication of the unchanging gospel has to adapt to the ever-changing needs of our culture and audience. We had used this as a defense for the unconventional, innovative methods we employed to communicate the gospel in our seeker days. And it makes sense to a point. We have technology available that Wesley did not have, so our methods will be different. But are the message and the methods we use to proclaim it really two distinct and unrelated issues?

As we began to understand the gospel of the kingdom, we questioned this split between message and method. There is a symbiotic relationship between the message and the methods we use to preach it—the methods we use are part of the message. The style and strategy of the church shapes the message that people hear.

I recently heard of a church that brought in acrobats to supplement their Christmas Eve services. Regardless of their actual role in the service, the presence of acrobats will shape the message heard. We will form ideas about God, the church and Christianity by watching acrobats fly through the air with the greatest of ease during a Christmas Eve service.

So we couldn't merely change the words we used to communicate the gospel because there were too many other messages ingrained in the Oak Hills culture that would contradict our words. Our fresh encounter with the gospel of the kingdom made us wrestle with some redemptively disruptive questions: Does the way we do church reinforce a theology of death to self? To what extent have we oriented our church around the needs of people who have minimal interest in actually living as disciples of Jesus? Is our ministry structured in a way that supports our conviction that church is more than Sunday services? Does the way we do church proclaim the gospel of life in God's kingdom? If someone attended our church for three months would he or she say discipleship is one of our central concerns?

As this message of the kingdom continued to sink in, we continued to unravel. We were slowly being pried loose from the firm grip of our own training and from beliefs that long ago had become malignant. Practically, this was crucial to the transition process. We could not hurry through it.

As in most churches, teaching is a critical component in shaping the overall culture of our congregation. Eventually we began to teach the gospel of the kingdom in our weekly messages. We didn't do it once in a while. For a season, virtually every sermon we gave attempted to communicate the wonder of the gospel of God's kingdom. The nonstop teaching gradually helped establish this gospel into the DNA of Oak Hills. But through the process we realized how deeply the various abridged versions of the gospel are entrenched in the minds of many Christians.

NONDISCIPLESHIP CHRISTIANITY

Nondiscipleship Christianity remains normative. People accept Jesus, but they don't trust him for much beyond the forgiveness of their sins. Their character, values, relationships and daily life remain unaltered by their devotion to Jesus. Christianity without apprenticeship is the predictable result of a truncated gospel that separates discipleship and salvation.

Not long ago I was in a conversation with several people from our church about the relationship between living out their faith and sharing it with those outside of God's family. At one point I asked, "What are the ingredients of a vital and life-giving Christian community that intrigues seekers?" Without hesitating, one woman responded, "Exclusivity." Everyone looked around the room thinking maybe she didn't understand the question. But in fact, she understood it perfectly.

By *exclusive*, she meant that there was something uniquely different about us as compared to the rest of the world. We are followers of
Jesus and that means we live differently. But *do* we live differently? As
we kept preaching the gospel of the kingdom we realized there were
hundreds of people in our church who considered themselves Christians but were not really interested in living as Jesus' disciples. Discipleship was available for those who were interested, but it wasn't
central to the message. People felt judged by our kingdom message.
They felt we were turning grace into works. They felt we were modi-
fying the "simple" gospel—Jesus died for our sins. We were up against
deeply entrenched ways of thinking about the gospel and the Christian life.

Our greatest challenge through the years of our transition was
dislodging the sin gospel from the hearts and minds of our people,
and from the culture of our church. Like trying to uproot a thick
weed, this was not easy. For many, the good news is that Jesus died
on a cross to take away our sins, and if we accept him as our Savior
we will go to heaven when we die. Obviously, this is true. The New
Testament teaches that Jesus came to "save his people from their
sins" (Matthew 1:21). The apostle Paul said,

> When you were dead in your sins and in the uncircumcision of
> your sinful nature, God made you alive with Christ. He forgave
> us all our sins, having canceled the charge of our legal indebt-
> edness, which stood against us and condemned us; he has taken
> it away, nailing it to the cross. And having disarmed the powers
> and authorities, he made a public spectacle of them, triumph-
> ing over them by the cross. (Colossians 2:13-15)

The gospel solves the problem of our sin and its collateral consequences. But the gospel is not only about sin and eternity. It has much
to say about who we can become and how we can live right now. It
has much to say about our lives today. The gospel invites us to a way
of living that trains us for eternity.

People willingly embraced the sin gospel. But they became nervous when we started teaching the gospel as a new way of living.

RENAMING WHAT WE ARE ALREADY DOING

As we continued to talk about the vision of life in God's kingdom, we had a front row seat on how people process things that don't align with their established beliefs. The kingdom of God phrase was confusing to many. They had not heard it much before, except as another way of talking about heaven. People wanted us to abandon the phrase and use language that was more familiar. Some tried to convert the kingdom language into more accessible ideas like "walking in the Spirit" or going "deeper into the Bible." They are part of the lectionary of the evangelical subculture. We think we understand what they mean, but it's an illusion. The real issue is not our comprehension but the way the code words and phrases make us think we are in control.

I remember a conversation with a woman who had heard one of our sermons explaining the gospel as life in the kingdom of God. She was unsettled by the fact that she had been a Christian for most of her life but had not heard the gospel explained this way. She grilled me for a simplified explanation of what it means. "You mean walking in the Spirit." "This sounds like Lordship salvation." She was trying to reclassify the unfamiliar into something she already knew, understood and had integrated into her life. I wanted to ease her restlessness. She is a godly woman. There probably isn't much material difference between living in the kingdom of God or walking in the Spirit. But this isn't about the meaning of words or phrases. It's about comfort and control. Old words and phrases reinforce entrenched thinking that may need to be loosened in order to fully embrace the kingdom gospel. At the end of his parable of the different seeds Jesus said, "Whoever has ears, let them hear" (Matthew 13:9). He knew our tendency to strain out what we don't like. He knew our ears weren't always used for hearing. We use them to sift out and sort through what doesn't align with how we already think and live. We use our ears to reinforce our preestablished positions. We hear what we want to hear.

THE PASTOR AS SPIRITUAL DIRECTOR

Meeting with people individually and in small groups was essential in the process of teaching the gospel of the kingdom to our church. People had questions and points to clarify, and it was vital for us to sit down with them and work out these issues. The endless demands of the seeker years had sharpened our leadership skills but perhaps dulled our skills as spiritual directors. In the seeker years we were busy planning creative services, meeting with a growing staff and making sure our programs were running efficiently. At some level, to preserve sanity, we were retreating from the "masses" and spending our time with the key leaders.

As we began to meet with people to help them understand the gospel of the kingdom, we rediscovered the importance of being spiritual directors to the people God had entrusted to us. We reengaged with the inner workings of the human soul, how it works and how God works in it. This was a critical discovery in our journey as a church. Kent and I recognized that our job was to wade into the details of a person's life and soul and bring God's wisdom. Too much distance from the specifics of what people are actually dealing with had made us professionals at programming events but amateurs at shepherding souls. The confusion surrounding our new understanding of the gospel put us back in front of people, and this individualizing continues to be an important part of our work.

THE NEED FOR A DECISION

The new language of living in God's kingdom made some of our evangelical friends uneasy for other reasons. They contended we were diminishing the centrality of the cross. We were minimizing the importance of making a personal decision for Christ. Eventually, they said, we had to admit our sin and accept Jesus as our Savior and Lord. The decision might happen in a moment or it might occur gradually over several years. But the decision had to be formalized by praying a prayer or being baptized or telling another about their faith.

Decisions are important. But perhaps praying a sinner's prayer or verbalizing our acceptance of Jesus was just a method, not a biblical prescription. Perhaps we needed the method to ease our anxieties over whether someone was actually "saved." When the gospel centers on forgiveness of sins and heaven after death, it is a neater package to set in front of someone. It's easier to seal the deal. Formal decisions are obviously good. At some point a decision has to be made to follow Christ or not. The question is, what constitutes a decision? Perhaps there are many ways people can demonstrate they have made a decision. Praying a prayer might be a good place to start. But as Kent and I began to understand the sweeping magnitude of the good news, we sensed God was bigger than our mechanisms for making a decision. Maybe the decision to trust Christ happens at baptism. Perhaps we simply start following Jesus' teaching in a specific area of life. Perhaps a woman is trapped in a tough marriage and decides to abandon her quest for control. She stops retaliating and applies herself to learning how to love. She learns the way of Christ and puts it into action in her marriage, even though she may not be able to articulate what she is doing. Suppose she does this without praying a sinner's prayer. Has she made a decision to follow Jesus? Again, it is good to formalize the decision. But the gospel of the kingdom invites us to trust God in everything. Trust is demonstrated by our willingness to act as though what we claim to believe is true. Some will begin their journey with Christ by getting on their knees, praying a sinner's prayer, and writing down the date, time and location in a journal. They will remember the experience for the rest of their lives. This is to be encouraged and celebrated. Others will, by the grace of God, begin living as though they really do trust Jesus and their "decision" will be woven into their new actions and choices. They will simply begin to orient their lives around Jesus. Their decision may be harder to dissect and identify, but it is no less real.

Sometimes memorable history begins with what seems at the time to be a small, even insignificant event. A parchment full of words nailed to the wooden door of a church; a lone woman who refuses to surrender her bus seat; two unknown reporters doggedly chasing a government cover-up. In our tiny little corner of the world called Oak Hills, discovering the gospel of the kingdom changed everything. Every aspect of our church was affected. It was our red pill. Once we accepted it, we couldn't go back. Jesus said, "The time has come. The kingdom of God has come near. Repent and believe the good news!" (see Mark 1:15).

5

CONSUMERISM

Talking to Fish About Water

KENT CARLSON

₡

With equal measures of resolve and dread, I sat across the restaurant table from a married couple in our church. Due to our church's change of direction (and undoubtedly some less-than-skillful handling of the process of change on the pastors' part), we had seen a startling exodus from our church over the last several years. This couple had written me to say they were leaving our church, and I decided to make an attempt to convince them to stay. Something had to be done to stem the tide of people leaving, and I was determined to do my part. Besides, I really liked this couple and honestly believed that if I could just spend enough time with them, they would change their minds. They were gracious enough to postpone their decision until we had a meal together and could discuss their concerns face to face.

We engaged in the obligatory small talk for a few minutes until we finally got down to the reason for our meeting. I told them that it was painful to hear they were leaving, and I wanted to know if there was anything I could do to change their minds. We spoke for a while about our church's change of direction, and they seemed to be, at least outwardly, pretty much in favor of that. Who wouldn't want to belong to a church that is seeking to help people orient their lives around the teachings of Jesus? So I asked, "Then why are you thinking of leaving? What's bothering you?" They mentioned two issues. They didn't like the responsive readings of Scripture in the worship services, and were bothered that we didn't have a Sunday school class for their high-school son.

I was dumbfounded and could not find the words to respond. I've been around long enough to know that presenting issues are not always the real or core issues. Still, this was their chance to tell their pastor what bothered them about the church, and they chose the responsive reading of Scripture and the lack of a high-school Sunday school class? I honestly didn't know what to say. As I mumbled a few comments in response to their concerns, I pictured my arms draped around their ankles as they walked away from our church. My attempt to convince this couple not to leave felt pathetic.

Again, I'm relatively certain that their presenting issues were not the core issues for them. They couldn't be, could they? I suspect these issues were just the hooks on which they hung their free-floating sense of discontent. Most likely they were being polite and didn't want to hurt my feelings, so they brought up the first thoughts that came to their mind. Still, I had an overwhelming sense that I didn't want to spend the rest of my ministry chasing people in this way. If this is what it would take to get people to stay at our church, I truthfully didn't have it in me.

But I knew the real issue had to go deeper than the particular likes or dislikes of the average person coming to our church. This was a wonderful couple, with a wonderful family, and they were simply making the kind of consumer decision that all of us make daily. How could it be otherwise? For a very long time we have been trained in our country to be consumers. We have an almost limitless amount of opportunities to consume. The entire economic system of our country is built on the consumption of goods that we, for the most part, don't really need. By the time our children reach elementary school, they are fully formed consumers. They look at their lives from a consumer perspective. Speaking to North Americans about consumerism is like talking to fish about water. It is an all-encompassing part of our daily existence and usually too close for us to even notice its pervasive presence.

DEVELOPING DEMANDING CONSUMERS

A few years ago I went to a day-long seminar led by a well-known business guru. We were in the middle of Oak Hills's rapid growth and nothing in my seminary training had prepared me for the challenges of being the leader of such a complicated and demanding organization. Like many of my pastor friends, I was willing to learn from the entrepreneurial giants of the world. Among the many principles this speaker presented, one stood out glaringly to me. He told us we should be "demanding consumers." He presented it as almost our patriotic duty. His reasoning was that our entire economy, and therefore our flourishing as a country, depends on companies and organizations that provide the very best goods and services at the lowest price. The dynamic that keeps this system running at peak efficiency is an army of demanding consumers who reward the best companies and punish those that perform poorly. It was economic Darwinism— the survival of the fittest. It was a perfect, symbiotic relationship between providers of goods and services and the consumer. Consumers demand, companies meet those demands, and everybody wins. This is the genius of capitalism. And the awful truth is that it works in the church in much the same manner.

As I reflected on this I realized that the issue isn't so much consumerism, because that is a fact of commercial American life we must learn to live with. The issue is that the church in North America has, for the most part, embraced this insidious monster of consumerism in the most pragmatic manner and has used it as a principle foundation for church growth. This truth came home powerfully to me in a conversation I had with a dear friend who is the pastor of another church in our town.

We were having one of our regular lunches together, and he brought up the name of a couple who had left his church for another. This couple had actually made the rounds, over the years, of several churches in town, including Oak Hills, but my friend was particularly bothered by this latest departure. And he made this rather interesting comment: "Kent, we should do something about this." Now I had been thinking a lot about these matters, and his suggestion fascinated me. I responded, "Well, I think I have the energy for one more good fight in me if you truly want to seriously address this issue. But if we're going to do a good job with it, we should really do a root cause analysis of the problem, but we might not like the answer we come up with. Because at the end of the day I believe we will discover that the problem does not lie so much with this couple and others like them, but with us. You're the problem." And then I added quickly, "And I'm the problem. We simply can't build churches around attracting people through all these religious benefits we offer and then be surprised when they actually take us up on it."

The difficulty is that we live in a church culture where external success is self-justifying. If more people are coming to our church, this is obviously a sign of success, and God must be pleased. The throng of people coming into the church is decisive evidence that the kingdom of God is advancing, or so we believe. And if this belief is held by the church leadership, then we will be continuously tempted to pursue pragmatic methods to attract and retain people. The insidious thing about this, of course, is that these efforts are inextricably enmeshed with teaching them how to follow Christ. In other words, our attractional methods are not value neutral. We are training people as we attract them.

I don't know how to say this in a gentle way, but we should not assume that those people who are attracted to our church have been captivated by the message of Christ and his alternative vision of life. In truth, most North American Christians are not riding courageously on warrior steeds with swords waving wildly in the air, crying out, "Let's change the world for Christ." Rather, they come in the air-conditioned comfort of their SUV or minivan with their Visa card held high in the air, crying out, "Let's go to the mall!"

We should be more truthful with each other here. They come because their high-school kid likes the youth program, or because their children don't get bored, or because they like the music, or because the pastor preaches the Bible the way they believe it should be preached, or because they happened to be greeted by a smiling face one day, or because the worship leader looks like Brad Pitt.

This is the hard, raw reality of life in the North American church. The people who come to our churches have been formed into spiritual consumers. This is who we are. It is our most instinctive response to life. And you can hardly blame us. Almost everything in our culture shapes us in this direction. But we must become deeply convinced that this is contrary to the teachings of Jesus Christ, the one who invited us to deny ourselves and lose our lives in order to find them. If we do nothing to confront this in our churches, we are merely putting a religious veneer over consumerism and nothing is changed. We offer no real, viable, attractive, alternative way of living. And what is worse, our churches become part of the problem. By harnessing the power of consumerism to grow our churches, we are more firmly forming our people into consumers. Pastors end up being as helpful as bartenders at an Alcoholics Anonymous convention. We do not offer what people really need.

HONESTLY WRESTLING WITH CONSUMERISM

As we began to teach (some would say relentlessly) about this at Oak Hills, we found ourselves running into all sorts of resistance. It was one thing to speak about consumerism in the abstract. Everyone agreed it was a thoroughly nasty and insidious thing. But when we began to push into very concrete and specific issues, that was another matter altogether. People began to push back. With some justification they complained that it seemed we were telling them not to have strong opinions about things. The truth is, all of us have our own laundry list of things we like and dislike, our specific tastes and preferences. Why wouldn't these preferences be valid in our church community? One woman said, with much frustration, "Kent, can't I have opinions about the kinds of songs we sing at church?" To which I replied, "Of course you can. It's perfectly fine to have opinions about all sorts of things. We all do. But perhaps we should not feel that our particular tastes and preferences should be catered to." After all, Jesus taught us to live well and be content even when we don't get what we want.

As we discussed the issue of consumerism, people asked how a follower of Jesus should decide which church to attend or keep attending. If it is not based, at least at some level, on a consumer decision, how else would one decide? For example, if I have children in high school, shouldn't I look for a church that has a healthy youth program? Or if I have a visceral dislike of loud, garage-band worship teams, can't I choose to attend a church that emphasizes hymns and more reserved music? These questions demonstrate how pervasive our consumer approach to life actually is. It is countercultural to consider making decisions on a basis other than how it benefits me.

Eugene Peterson has written a wonderful book titled *The Wisdom of Each Other* in which he creates a composite figure of the people he has given spiritual direction to over the years. In one letter to "Gunnar Thorkildsson," a late-in-life convert to Christianity, he writes:

> So, your friends are trying to turn you into a religious consumer, are they, inviting you to their wonderful churches where so much exciting stuff is going on? I would resist it. You're better off sticking with what you started out with at your Christian re-entry—the "smallest and nearest church." It's still my standard council in churchgoing. Of course, I admit exceptions, but not for the reasons your friends are setting out. Those several dozen phlegmatic Norwegians, dozing under the liturgical inexpertness of your young pastor, are as good company as any with whom to listen to God's word and worship his holy name. Where did all this frenzy in "looking for a good church" get started anyway? Certainly not from any passion for holy obedi-

ence among the "least of these my brethren." This church-shopping mentality, where we expect to find a flavor to suit every taste, is spiritually destructive. I don't see any good coming out of church worship that caters to our taste in worship.

As I see it, one of Peterson's points is that we become a part of a local church to have an encounter with the God who actually exists. And it must be a very small God indeed who can only be encountered at a church with a vibrant youth program, killer music and specialty coffee drinks in the lobby. Obviously, the danger is that we are choosing the church we attend not primarily to meet God but to satisfy our perceived needs. There is no way this can be good for our formation into the image of Christ.

I saw this with greater clarity at one of our regularly scheduled "Discover Oak Hills" meetings we have for people new to our church. I had each of the ten new people give a brief overview of their spiritual journey and what brought them to our church. Eight of them had come from the larger church down the street. That church was too large for their taste, and some of the other churches in town were too small. But they found our church just the right size. It reminded me of *Goldilocks and the Three Bears*. That church was too hard. The other was too soft. But this one is just right!

When it was my turn to speak I noticed that our pastor of community care had a worried look on her face. I suspect she was making a mental note of scheduling these meetings when I was unavailable. Regardless, I dove right in. After talking about the history and vision of our church for a few minutes, I spent some time talking about what it means to be a church family and that it's impossible to create authentic Christian community with people whose commitment is dependent on having their perceived needs continually met. I talked about the ancient Benedictine vow of stability. I described the church as being like a holiday gathering of an extended family where Uncle Fred always shows up drunk, Cousin Billy brings his latest floozy girlfriend, Aunt Martha gossips about everybody, and Grandma Helena adores everyone. The family may be incredibly weird, but it's still our family. People aren't skipping Christmas this year to be with the family down the street. We're family, and we learn to love each other, warts and all.

The funny thing is that most everyone agreed with what I said. They smiled at me and nodded their heads. How refreshing, they thought, to go to a church where the pastor speaks with such candor. But one delightful man in the group got it. I could tell by his face he was troubled. He was leaving his church and coming to ours primarily because we have a choir, which he wanted to join. "So," he said, "are you telling us to go back to the church we came from?" Our pastor of community care coughed nervously. "I wouldn't pretend to know what you should or shouldn't do. That's not my place," I said. "And I would so love for you and your family to be a part of the Oak Hills family. But what happens if, for some reason, we stop having a choir at Oak Hills and another church in town starts one up? Will you then leave us and go there? When does your church actually become *your* church?" I never saw this man again. I like to believe he went back to his previous church. If so, I think that is a good thing.

SUGGESTING A DIFFERENT PATH

What do we do about all this? How can we push back at something that is perhaps the most powerful force in American culture? As opposed to harnessing the power of consumerism to grow our churches, is there a way to deliver people from its insidious and soul-shrinking demands?

One thing we do is to simply teach on consumerism. Perhaps we taught too much about it. We began to get comments about how tired people were of hearing the word *consumerism*. If Mike or I would use the word in a sermon, we could almost sense a kind of collective eye-rolling. So we had to get sneaky about it. Instead of using the actual word we would say something like, "There is a pervasive value in the American culture that sucks all of us into believing that the world exists to meet our perceived needs. It is a ravenous, insatiable hunger that will permeate every square inch of our lives and drive us further from God and the experience of contentment." I felt like Treebeard the Ent, from Tolkien's *The Lord of the Rings*. It took us much longer to say some things, but we felt that we would not be faithful to the gospel if we ignored it completely.

I believe we must not give up on this. If consumerism is as pervasive as we believe, and if it is so contrary to the gospel of Jesus Christ, then we have to address it as skillfully and perhaps as provocatively as we can. Eugene Peterson addresses this head-on in his typically unapologetic and provocative manner:

> If we are a nation of consumers, obviously the quickest and most effective way to get them into our congregations is to identify what they want and offer it to them, satisfy their fantasies, promise them the moon, recast the gospel in consumer terms: entertainment, satisfaction, excitement, adventure, problem-solving, whatever. This is the language we Americans grow up on, the language we understand. We are the world's champion consumers, so why shouldn't we have state-of-the-art consumer churches? . . . There is only one thing wrong: this is not the way in which God brings us into conformity with the life of Jesus and sets us on the way of Jesus' salvation. This is not the way in which we become less and Jesus becomes more. This is not the way in which our sacrificed lives become available to others in justice and service. The cultivation of consumer spirituality is the antithesis of a sacrificial, "deny yourself" congregation. A consumer church is an antichrist church.

As pastors, one of our great responsibilities is to protect our flock from that which is spiritually harmful. And there is no more spiritually devastating force today than the antichrist spirit of consumerism. Much of the teaching of the New Testament will simply not make sense until "one has laid down the burden of having one's own way."

We can also push back at consumerism by not yielding to the temptation of attracting people from other churches to come to our church. As painful as this might be, we should gently and kindly suggest that it would be formationally beneficial for them to go back where they came from. When we try to attract people by intimating that our church offers something better than the other church, we are complicit in the whole sorry mess of consumer Christianity. We are now stuck in this wearisome game of keeping these people satisfied so they don't go to another church. Using terms popular in church-growth circles, once we have attracted them through the front door, we have to learn how to close the back door.

I know of a large church that lost over a thousand of their people to another large church in the same town. The "receiving church" celebrated this as a demonstration of God's blessing on their ministry. In my view this is a scandal that Christian leaders should speak against. How delightfully refreshing it would have been if the pastor of the "receiving church" had stood up one Sunday and preached a sermon on consumerism and invited those thousand people to humbly return to their previous church and meet God there. One can dream.

There is, though, one huge thing that we as Christian leaders can do about this sinister monster of consumerism, and that is to walk courageously into the unholy alliance that consumerism has forged with personal ambition. But that will take another chapter.

6

SETTING ASIDE AMBITION

The Necessary Groundwork of Change

KENT CARLSON

On my most optimistic days I find myself imagining opening up the latest issue of *Leadership Journal* and finding a panel discussion on the challenge of dealing with personal ambition. Five pastors of large, nationally known, outwardly successful churches are asked questions about their struggles with ambition. Their candor is a breath of fresh air. The dirty little demon of personal ambition is pulled out of the closet and laid naked on the table before everyone and exposed for the soul-destroying force that it is.

The pastors in this imagined article confess how much personal ambition has driven them and their ministries, and they give examples of some of the unattractive inner struggles they have with it. Issues of competition, jealousy, hunger for being known, thirst for personal significance, name-dropping, number-fudging, insecurities, gossip, being threatened by the success of others, a constant low-grade fever of dissatisfaction and looking for the next ministry buzz are discussed without any equivocation or rationalization. As we read, we can sense a gentle and redemptive humility in the panel's room. Tears begin to fall. There is repentance. They recognize that personal ambition has seriously harmed them, and they are disturbed by it. There is a collective realization that unbridled ambition is driven by the thirst to be "successful," which moves them away from the biblical call to faithfulness. There are moments of tender, truth-inspired silence as each pastor becomes increasingly aware that this has to change.

Going a little further with this thought experiment, I could imagine the huge impact a discussion like this would have on the evangelical leadership of our country. To have this dirty little secret of personal ambition exposed would foster a discussion on what is perhaps the most prevalent but least talked about pastoral sins. But for some reason Christian leaders are more candid about sexual lust than ambition. Yet it doesn't take a supernatural gift of discernment to know that ambition is there in embarrassing abundance.

THE ABSURD TRAP OF AMBITION

A few years ago, when many people considered our church "successful," I was invited to a small gathering of pastors of large churches. We were meeting to learn how to become more effective leaders. It was, admittedly, a heady few days for me. I got to mix it up with some of the bigger names and up-and-coming stars in the large-church subculture. As we began our meetings, there was an unmistakable sense that we had to establish the pecking order among us. It didn't take long to discern who had the largest church, which church was growing fastest, which pastor was better connected, who was more nationally recognized and so forth. At one level this is just basic social dynamics. It's the way the world works. The same dynamic occurs in a wolf pack. Only one wolf is the alpha male; everyone else falls in line. Still, all of us knew quite well that Jesus taught us that we were to do it a bit differently. If we wanted to become great, we must be a servant, and if we wanted to be first, we must be the slave of all (Mark 10:43-44). But there was nothing in the atmosphere of that meeting that encouraged Jesus' perspective. In truth, we were invited to this meeting because we were, even in our own little ponds, impressive. There were around thirteen of us. I figured I came in around ninth. I suspect this was somewhat delusional.

On the way back to the airport at the conclusion of this gathering, I grabbed a taxi with the pastor who considered himself at the very bottom of the food chain of impressive pastors. He was a bundle of insecurity and wonderfully authentic enough to admit it to me. He was three years into his church plant and had "only" 750 people coming to his church. He didn't feel he had the right to play with the big boys yet. Even back then, in my most ambitious days, I remember thinking that there must be something dreadfully wrong with a religious culture that would make someone as outwardly successful as this pastor feel insecure.

To complicate matters, it's easy to take potshots at successful pastors. They are easy targets who get shot at a lot. But the issue of personal ambition is only more obvious with them, not more real or more sinful. Those of us who look longingly and with envy at our successful colleagues are equally, if not more, guilty of ambition. The desire to be better than others, the odious nature of comparison and the lack of contentment with our actual state, is the problem formationally. This whole personal ambition thing is a very messy area.

Therefore, I walk into this subject of personal ambition with great apprehension. On the one hand, ambition is a robust and muscular virtue. It is the driving force behind many good and noble endeavors. Its absence would result in nothing much getting done in this world. When I reflect carefully on this, I realize that many, if not most, of the people I admire greatly have been highly ambitious. Ambition, in this sense, is a supremely necessary virtue for the flourishing of society.

On the other hand, it doesn't take much reflection to observe that ambition is often fueled by the insatiable desire to be recognized as important. Perhaps all we need to do, then, is to nurture good ambition and avoid the bad. If it were only that easy. My experience tells me that personal ambition is a ravenous monster not easily tamed.

And it is time to admit to each other that it runs rampant in the religious subculture of our day.

THE SHIFT FROM FAITHFULNESS TO PRODUCTIVITY

My observation is that over the last thirty or forty years our pastoral ethic has shifted from one of faithfulness to one of productivity and success. A generation of pastors and church leaders formed by the church-growth movement has slowly come to believe that our core pastoral mission is to build large and successful churches. Very few will actually admit this, but the truth is not hard to see. We have been trained to produce and "succeed," and we have learned our lesson well. When we carry this desire for productivity and success into a culture nurtured by the forces of consumerism and pragmatism, churches will be built around supplying religious goods and competing against other churches for the allegiance of the religious-consuming public. Instead of a particular brand of coffee or clothing line, we sell our various youth programs, worship styles and preaching abilities.

This shift in the pastoral ethic toward productivity and success has stirred the fires of personal ambition. Given the nature of our North American culture, this doesn't surprise me. How could it be otherwise? It also doesn't surprise me that the battle against this will be ferocious, for the tendency toward self-absorption plagues every one of us. Still, I wonder why this isn't more of a front-burner issue in popular Christian literature. We all know it's there. If only we could start speaking truthfully about it. And not by pointing to those naughty, self-driven pastors and church leaders out there someplace. We must begin with ourselves.

The struggle with personal ambition is, of course, not new. Paul tells us, "Do nothing out of selfish ambition or vain conceit. Rather, in humility value others above yourselves, not looking to your own interests but each of you to the interests of the others" (Philippians 2:3-4).

Through the centuries Christian spiritual giants have pounded away aggressively on this theme. For example, the Puritan divine Richard Baxter said: "Take heed lest, under the pretense of diligence in your calling, you be drawn to earthly-mindedness, and excessive cares or covetous designs for rising in the world."

There is no way to talk about pastoral ambition without sounding (and being, I suspect) judgmental. After all, who am I to know the thoughts and intentions of another person's heart? I am usually much deluded about my own. The inner motivations that drive all of us are a tangled web of sincerity and self-absorption, nobility and narcissism. We are seldom as bad as people say we are. Nor as good.

In addition, let me be clear that I would rather follow an ambitious pastor or church leader than a lazy one. Casual reflection on the life of the apostle Paul reveals a man of startling ambition who was powerfully used by God to change the world. I would rather follow someone who wants to change the world than one who simply enjoys throwing stones. Most of the pastors and church leaders I know are wonderfully sincere, hungry for God and bursting with integrity. They are largely motivated to make a difference for God. These men and women are in the trenches, punching it out in the often thankless grind of the impossible demands of leading a church. I know this firsthand. The men and women I have met in these ministries are some of the finest Christ followers our church culture has churned out. Almost exclusively, they are heroes, not villains.

But I write as one of those pastors. Over the past twenty-five years I have attended quite a few church-growth conferences that are offered in a major city on almost any given weekend. I've lunched with other pastors as we talked and evaluated what was going on. I observed as we sized each other up to see how quickly we could discover who had the highest attendance, the largest staff, the biggest budget, the most property, the newest book deal. The embarrassing secret that hardly anyone will admit is that these conferences are attended by those who, at some level, want to win at the game of who has the largest church. Or at least we want to make a good showing. Perhaps many who read these words will disagree with me, but I am convinced from direct experience, as well as paying close attention to the darkness of my own heart, that if thought bubbles suddenly appeared over the heads of those attending these conferences, we would all fall to the ground in repentance.

I am convinced that personal pastoral ambition, and a pastoral ethic centered around productivity and success, is brutal to our souls and destructive to the souls of the people we lead. We must become skilled at detecting the odor of personal ambition and then flee from it as if the church's future depends on it. I believe it does.

AMBITION AND CONSUMERISM

As I see it, there is a more insidious dynamic at play here than is often realized or admitted. Personal ambition has a symbiotic relationship with consumerism. The two go hand in hand. They feed off each other. As a Christian leader who is motivated by personal ambition, I can appeal to the basic consumer tendencies of the people I desire to be a part of my church or ministry. If I do this well, I will be rewarded by their attendance, their support and their allegiance, and my church or ministry will grow. Everybody is satisfied. Everybody gets what they want. The lighted match of my ambition ignites the dry timber of consumerism, and we have a raging fire that is very difficult to put out. While I suspect that there is not much that I can do about the cultural force of consumerism in our country, I believe I can do much about the forces that drive me as a Christian leader.

This uncomfortable truth about my own personal ambition is one of the first things I was confronted with during the Donner Party retreat (see chap. 2). At this retreat God graciously and kindly invited me to lay my ambition down. He invited me to learn how to do ministry without being driven by ambition. This has not been easy. In many ways I have been addicted to ambition, which means that withdrawal has not been enjoyable.

Admittedly, it was fun to be on the map, to be known as a successful pastor. I started receiving many invitations to speak. People actually wanted to learn from me. Church planters would ask me to give them the secret of my success. I wish I had been honest enough to simply suggest that all they needed to do in the 1990s was to get a sweetheart deal on a big piece of property in the middle of a small city that had no other large churches at the time and was adding thousands of new residents every month. Honesty would force me to admit that this is most likely the biggest secret to our "success."

A wonderfully sincere woman in our town once told me that the reason God had blessed our church, and the other large church in town, was because God knew we were the two pastors who could handle that success. She meant well, but I believe she was completely mistaken. I know many of the other pastors in our town intimately. They are, in many ways, far better pastors and human beings than I. I simply cannot bring myself to believe that our outward success was because I was more trustworthy. I only wish that were true. I do know I was ambitious, and not usually in the best way. And this had to change.

ADMIT THE PROBLEM

So what do we do about this? There is simply no way we will be able to purify all our motivations. Our most noble endeavors are tainted with sin and selfishness. We have to trust that as we pursue our interactive life with God, he will gradually and wonderfully transform our motivations and purify our ambition. This formational process should not stop us from giving ourselves "fully to the work of the Lord, because [we] know that [our] labor in the Lord is not in vain" (1 Corinthians 15:58).

There are, though, some areas that we can work at to declaw the monster of ambition. The first thing I would suggest (I know this sounds like it comes right out of some pop-culture self-help book) is that we have to admit that we have a problem. Try this. The next time you are with a group of pastors or Christian leaders, ask them if they ever struggle with personal ambition. You may have to be persistent, but if there is any sense of safety and trust in that group, eventually these leaders will start being painfully honest. My experience is that many pastors are tormented with a sense of inadequacy and live with a low-grade fever of envy. We are afraid we are not measuring up. We struggle to celebrate the successes of others. We desire to be known, recognized, important and significant, and we often use our church positions to pursue these false values. I believe it would be wonderfully healthy if we could admit this to ourselves and each other. Pull the little demon out of the closet and throw it on the table for everybody to see. Like most sins and character flaws, personal ambition thrives in secrecy and pretending. It's embarrassing to admit that we are insecure, and this insecurity fuels our ambition. A little embarrassment never hurt anybody.

FEAR AMBITION
Second, let's learn to fear ambition. It's true that there is a good and noble kind of ambition: the desire to get something done, to work hard, to leave a mark on the world, to make a difference. This is good. But I often hear Christian leaders say, "Perhaps I am ambitious, but I am ambitious for God." Well, maybe they are, but I find it curious that the vast majority of their ambition is directed toward the success of their own particular ministry. If we are ambitious for God, I suspect God may often have us giving ourselves with reckless abandon and boundless energy to something that neither brings us any recognition nor benefits our particular ministry.

Distancing ourselves from personal ambition is a crucial aspect of our spiritual formation. It is losing our life in order to find it. We resist this. We rationalize it, excuse it and ignore it. Life in the kingdom of God is about interior reality, about a hidden life with God, about a desire to decrease so that Christ may increase. The raw truth is that personal ambition keeps the story focused on us. This is why we should fear it. The kingdom of God does not always advance through outwardly impressive success. Jesus was clear about this. This should make us nervous, which would be good as well.

LINKING ARMS WITH OTHER MINISTRIES
Third, our churches can learn to place priority on cooperation with other ministries. I heard Dallas Willard once say that perhaps the

greatest hindrance to effectively reaching a community with the good news about Jesus is the division between churches in an area. This should be painfully obvious to us. In the New Testament we read about the church in Corinth, in Ephesus or in Philippi. The church where I pastor is in a town of close to seventy thousand people, and there are around thirty churches reaching about 20 percent of the population. Thirty churches trying to grow larger and literally competing with each other for the relatively small and stagnant percentage of people who are even remotely interested in the good news as it is currently proclaimed. Our community is not unique. This is the religious landscape of North America.

These are hard things to say, but if we were truly ambitious for God, we would have some frustration with the current migratory pattern of those who drift from one church to another. Whether we admit this or not, this accounts for the vast majority of church growth in our country, and it has very little to do with our mission of making disciples. In fact, if we were ambitious for God, we would probably pull out a "brood of vipers" sermon at least once a year, in which we would tell people to quit changing churches like they change cars (or spouses). We would work at creating a different kind of culture. Instead of advertising on Christian radio, we would make sure that the other churches in our area were blessed by our presence, not threatened. We would get to know other pastors, and would pray with them. We would put aside our own church's agenda from time to time and give ourselves to some other ministry or organization.

On a side note, it is a privilege for me to say that I actually live and minister in a town where a small cadre of pastors work very hard at this. These men and women have a larger kingdom mindset. We love being together and have met weekly for prayer and horsing around for over twenty years. We represent churches of various shapes and styles, from the very large to the very small. We have joint services and go on retreats together. We have walked through the highs and lows of life and ministry together. We live in each other's hearts. I would be lost without them and am deeply grateful for them.

HELPING THE AMBITIOUS PASTOR

My fourth suggestion is not primarily about the pastor but the leaders and members of the church. The competitive church environment that we have developed in North America has created a kind of children's game of "my pastor can beat up your pastor." Admittedly, we pastors have been complicit in this game, but the average layperson has played a part as well. Every pastor I know has had those excruciating conversations with a church member who explains why he or she is leaving for the "Church of What's Happening Now" down the street. The reason, while usually couched in polite religious language, is essentially that the other church and the other pastor offer a better product. The departing family does not feel they are "being fed" and are looking for a church and a pastor who will more adequately meet the needs of their family.

It doesn't take much psychological sophistication to realize the dynamic created in that kind of an environment—performance. In order to maintain the relationship, the pastor has to perform at a certain level and in a certain way in order to continue to receive the support and involvement of the church member. While this may work well for a restaurant or a department store in our North American economic system, it is destructive for a community of faith. The best metaphor for church community is the healthy family, not the marketplace. It is psychologically damaging for a spouse or child to live in a home where a certain level of performance is required in order for the relationship to be valued. When a relationship is conditional, deep and abiding love and community can't be created and maintained.

The same is true of the church. We all know this. And because of performance demands, many pastors struggle with a growing cynicism, or at least a kind of disengaged distance. We know that those who love and praise us today are often the ones who will be leaving us tomorrow.

Please understand that I am not suggesting that church members should simply ignore their concerns or criticisms about the church and its ministries. It's quite obvious that pastors and churches are filled with flaws and shortcomings. And often the critiques and perspectives and opinions of disgruntled laypeople are dead-on accurate, presenting a needed corrective to a church's ministry. But this can be pursued in the context of a committed relationship. It is one thing to sit down with an upset person who I know is not going to leave the church. It's another thing altogether for someone to use the threat of leaving as a kind of hammer to get what they want.

I raise this issue because much of the fuel for pastoral ambition comes from the pressure to attract and keep the support of the people in the church. And again, pastors are certainly complicit in allowing this dynamic to flourish. But a word to the concerned layperson is appropriate here.

I recently was with a pastor friend who has been in the same church for over two decades. He is a beautiful human being who deeply loves the people in his church. His ministry has not been an easy one. Many have left his church over the years to populate the other churches in the area. There has been a low-grade discontent in his church that he has had to live with for years. And yet this man has been a rock in his community. He is tremendously respected and loved by many inside and outside his church. One day I asked him if he thought his church realized how deeply loved and respected he was by so many people. He looked at me and couldn't speak for a few moments. The pain he felt was raw and deep. It was almost as if he could never do enough for them.

Laypeople might be tempted to think that the way to rescue pastors from ambition is to not let them think too highly of themselves. Just keep reminding them in no uncertain terms that their feet are made of clay. I greatly disagree. In fact, I would go in a completely different direction. Let your pastors know you love them. Let them know that you are in this relationship for the long haul. Let them know that even when you disagree, even when you are angry, even when they fail, the relationship is still strong and secure. I suspect that at the core what most pastors fear is not failure but rejection.

EMPHASIZE THE TRUE PURPOSE OF THE CHURCH

Fifth, if we were ambitious for God and not for ourselves, we would emphasize the *purpose* of our churches rather than organizational success. From my perspective the commission Jesus gave us is about making disciples, which is not primarily about decisions for Christ, forgiveness of sins or heaven when we die. Making disciples is excruciatingly more difficult than growing a church. It is a wonderfully inefficient process that does not often lend itself easily, especially in our North American culture, to mass production. It would be wonderful if the strategic thinking and leadership muscle so prevalent in large-church circles were more intentionally pursuing this goal. This should be our noble ambition. Perhaps the results of this pursuit might be less impressive outwardly. We may even have to get leaner and meaner in order to make disciples. It would take no small amount of courage and resolve to pursue this route.

I am convinced that we have trained Christians to be demanding consumers, not disciples. If you doubt this, as an experiment try scaling down the services at your church for three months to just prayer and Scripture reading and watch what happens. If this is too frightening, just imagine doing it. What do you think would happen? Once we have created the monster, it never stops demanding to be fed. Consumers demand that we deliver the goods or they will take their business elsewhere. Though this is the creative force behind capitalism, it has little to do with following Christ.

In my more optimistic and hopeful moments, I imagine an army of Christian leaders willing to unplug from this consumer-entrepreneurial model and linking arms to pursue our calling to make disciples of Jesus. Perhaps few would follow us, and from an external perspective we might look like failures, but it would be an honorable pursuit. I, for one, am simply bored of trying to satisfy the often absurd demands of the church-going public. It actually seems somewhat demeaning to me. Maybe a rebellion is exactly what is needed.

REDUCE OUR EXPOSURE

Sixth, there is no way we can reduce our personal ambition without reducing our public exposure. There is a reason that celebrities are so often messed up. Seeing our faces and names everywhere is bound to give us a warped understanding of ourselves, the world and our place in it. We must learn to crave obscurity. At times we must literally hide. We must give ourselves to small and insignificant deeds that nobody knows about. And then must resolve to never humbly work them into a sermon.

It is dangerous for us to find ourselves receiving a certain degree of notoriety for our leadership endeavors. This too we should fear. Many people in our churches experience vicarious pleasure from knowing that their pastor is relatively well known, successful and popular. This is not only spiritually unhealthy for them and us, it is weird. We should do what we can to avoid this. If we must have photos published of ourselves, we should use recent ones that actually look like the saggy middle-aged man or woman we have become. We can follow up impressive public events with seasons of obscurity and menial tasks. We can visit at the local convalescent hospital. We can clean a toilet.

THE AMBITION TO DECREASE

John the Baptist is a wonderful example for us. He was the main show in town until Jesus came along. Then people stopped following John and started following Jesus. It had to bother him. It's hard to give ground, to decrease, to have our personal ambition exposed and then to die to it. But if we don't learn this, we fail the gospel, our people and ourselves.

In the final analysis ministry is not about our outward success. It is not a numbers game. If our organization is growing while the actual percentage of nonchurched people in our area remains the same, we are not accomplishing our mission. If our communities are not dramatically influenced by the churches in our area, we are not living out our faith in any radical way. If followers of Christ are barely distinguishable from the nonchurched people around us, the kingdom of God is not advancing.

When we reflect on all this, perhaps ambition is needed more than ever. But it must be ambition directed toward something other than personal and organizational success. We must be ambitious to decrease so Christ may increase. This is truly something worth giving our lives to.

7

CO-PASTORING

Two Are Better Than One

MIKE LUEKEN

❧

I moved to California in 1995 to be the pastor of an Oak Hills–sponsored new church plant. I was excited about the challenge and was determined to do it all and do it successfully. I was hungry for the opportunity. I remember sitting at dinner with a handful of denominational leaders conveying my passion to advance God's cause and build his church. I knew I was speaking their language. In some way, I also knew I was posing. Church planting was a challenge, but I was confident I could do the job. Sort of.

Before leaving my previous assignment, a friend spoke the truth to me. He thought my ego was the driving force behind my decision to leave. His words were hard to hear. I couldn't receive what he was saying. But I knew, in some distant place within me that I couldn't access, he was right. My defensive reply should have been a clue. A few years later I was able to admit it. "Stardom and individual heroism," to use a phrase from Henri Nouwen, contributed to and perhaps even drove my decision to plant a church.

Henri Nouwen writes:

When you look at today's church, it is easy to see the prevalence of individualism among ministers and priests. Not too many of us have a vast repertoire of skills to be proud of, but most of us still feel that, if we have anything at all to show, it is something we have to do solo. You could say that many of us feel like failed tightrope walkers who discovered that we did not have the power to draw thousands of people, that we could not make many conversions, that we did not have the talents to create beautiful liturgies, that we were not as popular with the youth, the young adults, or the elderly as we had hoped, and that we were not as able to respond to the needs of our people as we had expected. But most of us still feel that, ideally, we should have been able to do it all and do it successfully. Stardom and individual heroism, which are such obvious aspects of our competitive society, are not at all alien to the church. There too the dominant image is that of the self-made man or woman who can do it all alone.

I was about to experience the agonizing wisdom of Nouwen's words.

THE CHURCH I NEVER PLANTED

I spent the first year in California serving at Oak Hills in a variety of capacities. I was also trying to get Rock Creek Community Church off the ground. Inspired by the title of John Ortberg's *The Life You've Always Wanted*, I could write a really short book titled *The Church I Never Planted*.

The church never got traction. After about eighteen months, I made the excruciating decision to shut down the fledgling church and accept a permanent position at Oak Hills. The entire ordeal was extraordinarily difficult. But God used this adventure to further advance the meticulous, painful process of "ego demolition."

I officially began serving at Oak Hills in 1997 as the spiritual formation pastor. I was responsible for the midweek worship service and the discipleship ministry. It was a fun, adrenaline-filled season in our history. The church was thriving. I felt like I was growing as a leader.

CO-PASTORING

In the summer of 2001 Kent asked me how I felt about being a co-pastor with him. I was intrigued by the possibility of what this might look like and how it might work. But I was also apprehensive. Kent was the founding pastor. He'd been at Oak Hills for eighteen years at that point. He is a gregarious leader. He is an engaging, humorous communicator. People enjoy his personality. He knows how to work a crowd. The church loves him.

Because of the differences in our personalities, I knew it would be hard for me to carve out my own space. There would be constant comparisons. I wasn't looking forward to the myriad of identity questions that I knew would arise within me. It would take vigilance to fend off these attacks. I was also concerned about the artificiality factor. My crap detector works pretty well. Titles don't create roles.

In spite of these concerns the idea still felt good to me. I loved the people and culture of Oak Hills. It was unlike any church I had seen or even imagined might exist. The people accepted me and responded well to my style. At the time Kent asked the co-pastoring question, we had, for a few years, shared the leadership of the church. He was the point person for the outreach/seeker emphasis, and I led the discipleship/New Community emphasis. We collaborated on key decisions. We spent many hours in each other's offices, dialoguing on important issues. We both sat on the elder board. We shared the leadership role with the staff. The fact that we had functioned as co-leaders for years made the whole idea more legitimate. Co-pastoring was not a declaration of what we were going to do but of what we were already doing. Our elder board supported the idea. We announced our intentions to the staff and church in the fall of 2001.

Over the last several years we've had the opportunity to share the Oak Hills story at various conferences and seminars. In each of these settings we have talked about our co-pastoring relationship. For many reasons it is a critical element of the story. Each time we have talked about it, we've found people skeptical of how it actually works. They don't believe two people can actually be the co-leaders. It's not that the concept is foreign. People have written and talked about co-pastoring for a number of years. It's an attractive idea on paper. But we've found people doubt it actually works.

And I love the skepticism. It forces me to sharpen my thinking. It makes me face some of the ugly stuff in my own heart.

People assume that someone ultimately is in charge. Regardless of titles, people think there really is just one primary leader, one senior pastor. Ironically, this is what caused me to pause from the very beginning.

MAKING CO-PASTORING WORK

As time has passed, there are a number of key elements to our relationship that make it work.

Willingness to release power. One reason our co-pastoring works is because of Kent's rigorous pursuit of his own spiritual formation. He has done a marvelous job of empowering my leadership. When I have recommended a course of action, he has always been attentive and willing. When I disagree, he listens. When I cast vision, he follows. When I suggest a new approach, he gets excited. When I raise a concern, he thinks it through. He has done a wonderful job of creating space for me to shape the landscape of our church. He was the one who had to be willing to surrender some control and power. He has repeatedly let it go. As a result we each have our role. We each influence the church and each other. We both shape the culture of our church.

At the same time, Kent is the founding pastor. He's been at Oak Hills for twenty-five years. He's ten years my senior. So I realize that, in many ways, Kent is "more" the senior pastor than I am. In some respects the church does look to him as their primary leader. He officiates at most of the weddings and funerals. He meets with the other pastors in the community. He has a platform that I don't have. But he has never trumped my leadership by playing that card.

Mutual respect. Another reason the arrangement works is because we have so much in common. We both love Oak Hills. We believe the gospel is about new life. We believe transformation is possible. We both tend toward the ironic and the absurd. We both have a dark side. The Christian subculture makes us squirm. We are on the same page with most things that matter.

But co-pastoring also works because we greatly respect and value our differences. We are very different people. Kent is from Chicago and is a Bears fan. I'm from Wisconsin and am a Packers fan. I have more reasons to cheer than he does. Every spring he believes the Cubs will win the World Series. I think baseball is boring. Kent is an off-the-charts extrovert. I'm an introvert. He can work a crowd. I prefer a small group. He processes his thoughts verbally. I mull things over. He makes decisions quickly. I ponder all the options. He's fifty-seven. I'm forty-seven. He watches offbeat, independent films. I watch old, classic movies. He is a microbrew snob. I'm content with Coors Light. Kent would do well in an urban setting. I'm more at home in the suburbs. We learn from each other. We sharpen each other. Our differences have made us better men, better Christ followers and better pastors. Combined, we give the church a far better and more diverse pastor than either one of us could be on our own.

This may sound a little strange. (I feel like Dr. Phil.) Our co-pastoring often seems like a marriage. In some ways it is. To the extent that it is, Kent is the wife. (Note from Kent: This is obviously not true. I have a beard. [Response note from Mike: If Kent were more spiritually formed, he would not need to defend himself here.]) We have worked together for fifteen years, half of that time as co-pastors. But co-pastoring is not a paradigm we have permanently adopted at Oak Hills. If one of us were to leave the church, we would not hire a new co-pastor. Our differences are real and many. But we deeply value and highly respect who the other is and the gifts he brings to the table. More than being co-pastors, we are committed friends.

Deep friendship. Our friendship has been forged through years of hard work, shared experience and spending time together. On many occasions we've sat around fires and shared our pain with each other. We've talked about our dark side. We've been brutally honest about challenges in our marriage or with our children. We've entrusted our deep insecurities with each other. We've confessed our sins. We've been able to confide in each other without fear of job repercussions. We've also walked with each other through personal difficulties. Co-pastoring works because we trust and believe in each other. That doesn't mean we don't question each other. Nor does it mean it's always been smooth sailing. But at the end of the day, we trust each other. We believe in each other. Our strengths complement each other's weaknesses. Ultimately, the arrangement works because our friendship is stronger, and more important to us, than the "success" of the church.

Splitting responsibilities. Functionally, we share the preaching and teaching responsibilities. Over the course of a year, we each speak about 50 percent of the time. We divide the rest of our church responsibilities in half. We lead our areas and provide input to one another about the overall ministry. Kent is responsible for the weekend services, worship, communications, compassion, missions, elder board, and facilities and finances. I lead spiritual formation, small groups, evangelism, children and youth, and women's and men's ministries. If one of us is gone because of a vacation or outside responsibility, the other provides the leadership wherever it is needed.

Shattering the celebrity syndrome. Co-pastoring has forced our people to be less attached to one personality or voice. This helps people receive the message without becoming enamored with the messenger. In larger churches the celebrity status of the senior pastor creates a situation where religious consumers are pulled by their whims and preferences. They want a senior pastor who is funny. They want him to be a *him*. They want him to preach verse by verse through the Bible. They want a friendly pastor who will stand at the back of the auditorium and shake their hands as they leave. They want him to visit them in the hospital. They want someone who remembers their name. This is perhaps a basic desire in all of us to be noticed and cared for by people in power.

But this incessant craving for satisfaction puts impossible pressure on the pastor. Henri Nouwen was right in saying that pastors often feel like they don't have what it takes to fulfill their calling, but they still feel the pressure to do it all and do it successfully. It's a black hole of discouragement. Co-pastoring is a spiritual discipline that confronts the consumerism of our congregation.

On the flip side, when things are difficult, people want to know who to criticize and blame. I suppose we all feel better when we can isolate the cause of the turmoil. When the Bears are losing, it's easier and more cathartic to blame Jay Cutler. If the Cubs are losing, it's time to fire the manager. Co-pastoring has enabled us to spread the complaints and criticisms across two sets of shoulders. This has reduced the degree of angst we have had to carry.

OVERCOMING THE DIFFICULTIES
But there are challenges to this arrangement.

Inherent inefficiencies. Because there are two point leaders, there is a degree of redundancy and inefficiency. Conversations often happen twice. Staff has to get input from two different people. Kent and I have to make sure we are keeping each other up to speed on what's happening and what we're thinking so we don't get too far ahead of the other. To lead our areas well, the other guy has to be onboard. Sometimes this takes a ton of time and energy. Our staff has pulled their hair out trying to navigate two leaders with different styles and different ways of handling any given situation. If each were leading his own church, the daily operation and flow would be smoother. The co-leading arrangement makes it difficult to operate at peak capacity and maximum productivity.

Crowded leadership space. Closely related is the tendency we have to yield to the other; we don't always lead at full capacity. There is only a certain amount of leadership room. Kent is particularly sensitive to my desire for space to lead, and works hard to give me that space.

When we are both on top of our game, assertively leading, we bump into each other. This can be awkward and uncomfortable. It creates tension. At times it produces conflict. It can happen at the microlevel of an elder board meeting. It can happen at the macrolevel of assessing the temperature of the church or trying to discern what values or objectives need attention. To avoid the weirdness of bumping into each other, we stand back and yield to one another. We are both acutely aware of the reality of this exhausting dynamic. It is something we openly talk about. We are both so concerned about getting in each other's way, we let the other take the lead, but sometimes neither one of us does. This is just one of the complicated and goofy aspects of co-pastoring. Over the years we've worked hard to keep communication open and honest in order to minimize the inefficiency.

Dealing with conflict. Anyone in a leadership position understands how his or her attitude trickles down and shapes the rest of the organization. The way we talk about a challenge, our level of optimism, our enthusiasm—these flow from the leader directly into the organization's culture. In a co-pastoring situation there is the added factor of the relationship between the two leaders. The church subconsciously sees our interaction in the front row before a service. They read between the lines of our relationship. If we are having fun and getting along, they feel good. If we are struggling and discouraged, they are concerned. (Again, the strange marriage metaphor, with the congregation as the kids.)

Over the years Kent and I have had our share of disagreements. We are strong leaders with strong opinions. We don't see every issue the same way. There are times when we disagree with how the other is handling a situation. Several times the fabric of our friendship has been tested by the demands of leadership and the complexity of co-leadership. The conflict is inevitable. One of the biggest challenges of co-pastoring is learning how to redemptively wade into and talk through the conflict. It takes boldness. We have to be willing to endure the sometimes suffocating weirdness. Both of us are comfortable and fairly skilled in difficult conversations. We have them often with staff and people in the church. But we hesitate with each other.

Many times in the past decade, there have been instances where the tension was mounting between us. We needed to get in a room, lock the door and talk it out until we could let it go. But for whatever reason, we didn't walk into the conflict as assertively as we should have. Perhaps our insecurities got in the way. I suspect we each have baggage from our past that is exposed in our conflict with each other. Our weaknesses meet each other and paralyze us. Our elder board has witnessed this dynamic between us. They have encouraged us to figure it out for the sake of our friendship and the health of the church. While we have worked hard at this, communication around conflict management continues to be a growth area.

A SPIRITUALLY FORMATIVE STRUCTURE

Nouwen was right when he said, "stardom and individual heroism . . . are not at all alien to the church. There too the dominant image is that of the self-made man or woman who can do it alone." One of the dangers of the sole senior pastor, particularly in a larger church, is the ego stroke that comes from being "the man." We call the shots and make the key decisions. We have "administrative assistants." We have a separate phone line into our office. People tell us we are great communicators. The power is intoxicating. Our false selves drink deeply from the fountain of flattery and praise.

It's not that co-pastors are beyond these temptations. But the structure of co-pastoring is safer than doing it alone. Inherent in the structure is the realization that we can't "do it all and do it successfully." We've stressed the priority of spiritual formation throughout this book. For Kent and me, co-pastoring has been the most spiritually formative force in our lives for the past decade. By far. It has confronted our ambition, ego and need for approval. It has stripped away some of the shaky scaffolding on which we build our ministries. It has taught us to trust God to be at work in the unfolding of a process. It has taught us to trust each other. Mostly, being the co-leaders of the church has forced us to deal with not always getting what we want.

This is absolutely crucial in a culture of consumerism. Countless times Kent and I have had to surrender our personal leadership agenda and preferences. We've had to practice the discipline of submission to each other. Without this, the co-pastoring would have blown up years ago.

Mutual submission is what makes this work. It's been the key ingredient since the beginning. Kent never felt the need to hold onto the leadership of the church, and I never felt the need to grab it. He was able to let it go, and I was able to receive it. Co-pastoring has been a decade-long adventure in learning what it means to live in humility and mutual submission. This has been profoundly beneficial for our souls and those at Oak Hills.

We would not have endured the grind of the last decade without each other. There were too many changes, too many complaints, too many people leaving and too many unanswerable questions. We have been humbled and honored to navigate this decade of change as the co-leaders of our church.

8

UNDERSTANDING THE CHURCH

The Fellowship of the Unformed

MIKE LUEKEN

ᒿ

*A*dmittedly, this was one of those sappy incidents pastors notice and then ruin by using it in a sermon. So forgive me in advance. It was Communion Sunday. I was in the back of the auditorium reveling in the scene of hundreds of people filing forward to partake of the bread and the cup. It is sacred to watch people receive the sacraments. For some, it takes all the faith they have just to walk forward. They come hoping to meet Jesus. Some understand the celebration better than others. Some are actively seeking God and the life he has for them. Others are just trying to stay on God's good side. Some people think they are holier than they are. Others know they have a penchant for particular sins. Communion is quite the parade of souls. But it always increases my faith to see people at varying degrees of spiritual passion and commitment receiving it. In ways I don't fully understand, it stirs me to know people are seeking God and, perhaps more importantly, he is seeking them.

On this particular Sunday I noticed a young family near the back of the room begin to walk forward. The mom and dad are active in our church and regulars at our services. They worship with their five-year-old son and three-year-old daughter by their side. The little girl caught my eye because she was wearing bright red boots that looked like they would transport her home if she clicked them together. As she walked toward the Communion line, she sucked her thumb and twisted her hair. Though the service wasn't nearly over, she was ready for her afternoon nap. The young boy held a tattered stuffed animal by its ragged arm. This young family was coming to meet Jesus and remember his sacrifice. Communion, for the children, was undoubtedly a midmorning snack to partially satisfy their hunger. They didn't understand what they were doing. But they were coming, and Jesus was there. Some suggest children should not receive Communion until they reach the age of understanding. Perhaps. But what is the age of understanding? I'm forty-seven and I don't understand the mystery of Communion. The illusion of understanding pinches the mystery of faith. Perhaps children are actually better prepared to receive Communion because they come in humility and honesty without any pretense that they know or understand more than they do.

As the family made their way forward, the little boy, with a delightful grin on his face, suddenly stopped. In what seemed like slow motion, he bent over and did a somersault. With joy on his face, he got up and got in line for Communion.

After receiving the elements the family went to the back of the auditorium and huddled together for a few minutes. I noticed the dad trying to explain the significance of the bread and the cup. They began to pray. I was watching the little boy as he opened his eyes in the middle of the prayer and with that same infectious smile guzzled his cup of juice. Apparently he was thirsty. Dad was droning on, and the boy wanted a drink. He didn't wait for the prayer to end. He drank the cup before he ate the bread. He broke the Communion "rules." The whole scene was sacred to me.

This is the church. Humble. Unrefined. Family. People who are at different points on the journey. The church is people who are battered by life and want God. It's also those who are going through the motions. It's people with only enough faith to stand up and walk forward, hoping God will meet them. It's those who understand, at least partially, what it means to follow Jesus. But it's also those who don't understand and really don't care. The church is people who choose joy even when life is hard. It's people who complain. It's a spectrum of people with different degrees of spiritual hunger and motivation. The church is messy, unfinished and imperfect. But the church is the beloved bride of Christ.

As we continued to transition to being a church that prioritizes spiritual formation, we came to a different understanding of its role in God's work of establishing his kingdom on earth as it is in heaven. This shift was brought on, ultimately, by our new understanding of the gospel. Because it was primarily conceptual and theological, this shift is only partially reflected in actual programs or practical examples.

REVISING THE MISSION STATEMENT

During our decade as a seeker-targeted church, our mission statement was "to turn nonchurched people into fully devoted followers of Jesus Christ." It was not a unique mission, but it was audacious. We wanted to change our corner of the world with the message of Jesus. We passionately wanted to reach seekers with the gospel. The core people of our church understood the mission and their part in the strategy. We were unified around this shared cause of reaching our community, and it was exhilarating to be part of something that was making a difference. We constantly reminded our people that the church is the hope of the world. The Great Commission is worth the sacrifice of our time, talents and money.

But as we began transitioning, we started asking questions about the broader purpose of the church. We were becoming suspicious of numerical growth as an infallible indicator of God's endorsement and blessing. We considered the *way* we were doing church, not only the results we were seeing.

We spent long meetings with staff, elders and people from the church unpacking various tensions. For example, the tension between the church as a viable organization that is accomplishing goals, and the church as an alternative community that operates by an agenda and set of values foreign to this world. The church fueled by a compelling mission but also a place where the story of God is continuously retold. The church's need for strong leadership that trusts God with the outcomes.

As we grappled with these tensions, we grew increasingly uneasy with the muscular language of our mission statement. "Turning nonchurched people into fully devoted followers of Christ" rolls off the tongue nicely and is easy to remember. But the hard-driving, hill-climbing, change-the-world flavor didn't fit us anymore. More important, though, the mission did not reflect our spiritual formation priority. Obviously we wanted to continue to reach lost people and develop disciples. But the language of our mission statement was inextricably linked to the strategy and style we had used to fulfill it.

After many conversations and prayers we decided to rewrite our mission statement to better reflect who we are. This was another DNA-altering decision. It drove the stake of who we are and where we are heading deeper into the ground.

Our new mission statement is "to invite people to experience the reality of life in the kingdom of God." Our job was to invite people to new life in Jesus, but the Spirit of God had to make it happen. We couldn't turn anybody into anything.

We wanted our mission statement to reflect our desire to be a church that helped people develop a conversational, interactive relationship with Jesus. Because of our conviction about the gospel of the kingdom we wanted a mission statement that celebrated the possibility of a new life under God.

We knew a change in mission might further accelerate the exodus from Oak Hills. It would certainly validate concerns about leadership angst and instability. But we were not the same church. Our mission

had changed whether we wanted to publicly admit it or not. Eventually, we introduced the new mission statement to the congregation. It
met mixed reviews.

As expected, many were not invested enough in the church to care
about the language of our mission statement. Those who had hoped
we would snap out of our funk and return to our seeker style now
realized we weren't turning back. The kingdom of God language confused many people. Others were not clear on what they were supposed to do. But the intriguing language of life in the kingdom of God
and the possibility of transformation piqued others' curiosity. More
specifically, newer Christians who were not yet assimilated into the
Christian subculture were drawn to this mission. We also began noticing that seasoned Christ followers who were weary of a faith without transformation were encouraged by a mission statement that
raised the possibility of Jesus actually making a difference in their
daily lives.

REDEFINING SUCCESS
When we were in the midst of our transition, I attended a conference
where I reconnected with an old friend. As we were catching up with
each other, he asked me how our church was doing. I reluctantly
began to explain the complicated, confusing and sometimes painful
journey we had been on. While he periodically nodded his head in
understanding, I knew he didn't. He couldn't. To get it, we would
have needed to pull up two chairs and have a long, unhurried "deck"
conversation. Instead, he cut to the chase and asked me the mother of
all questions: "Is the church growing?"

It was a fascinating moment. I was droning on about the various
twists and turns in the journey of our church, trying to explain what
had occurred in all of its glorious subtlety and complexity, and he
wanted to know if the bottom line was red or black. A black bottom
line meant the journey was worth it. A red bottom line meant it
wasn't. In that brief conversation, I saw one more time how American
ideals have profoundly shaped our ecclesiology.

The attendance at our church was in a free fall for years. It's hard to write about the perils of outward success without it sounding like sour grapes. But when attendance was declining, our elder board spent many hours rethinking what it meant for us to succeed as a church. We concluded that faithfulness to the gospel might mean outward failure. The biblical story was filled with supporting evidence.

"Is the church growing?" This question hovers in the minds of honest church leaders. But it hardly feels like a question. It's more like a taunt or a test.

Answering yes means more people are coming to the services. Attendance is rising. The church's efforts are "working." The leadership is competent. We pass the test. We are succeeding. God is on our side. He is blessing us.

Answering no means the opposite.

Yes is said with confidence.

No is mumbled.

Yes is tempered by disingenuous, self-deprecating statements: "We don't really know what we are doing." "I'm just a simple man, so this growth is hard to understand." The country bumpkin shtick is well meant, except it is contrived and dishonest.

No is qualified with "but" statements.

It is a fascinating game we play.

Periodically a list of the fastest-growing churches in America is published. I suspect America is one of the few places in the world where "fastest-growing" is the unquestioned metrics of success. If the attendance graph is steadily going up, then God must be on the move. If it is going down, we must be doing something wrong. The leaders of the "fastest-growing" churches are invited to speak at conferences. They are the ones we want to hear from. They are the ones who have figured something out the rest of us need to discover. What would happen if the keynote speaker at the next national conference was the associate pastor of a sixty-person church in rural Nebraska who hasn't had a visitor in five years? It's just a hunch, but registrations might lag. We love the theory of lessons learned in struggle and failure. But the reality is not nearly as attractive.

Mark Galli writes:

Many pastors and lay leaders recognize that they are in a superficially successful church, and that it's time to introduce the harder edges of the gospel. But how? How do we get comfortable people to listen to a gospel that includes a lot of discomfort? How do you deepen discipleship without introducing despair? How do you insist firmly on faithfulness without becoming legalistic? Most important, how do you manage the loss in membership? That will happen. The more strictly you adhere to the teachings of Jesus, the smaller the church will "grow." One of the most crucial skills of a military commander is, in the face of defeat, to lead a retreat that doesn't turn into panic or a massacre. And one of the most crucial skills for pastors and church lay leaders is to manage church decline when people are leaving because they see, finally, what Jesus is asking of them. This is not a job for the faint of heart, and will require great wisdom to manage resources, personnel, and morale in such a time. Evangelicals have become the unmatched experts in church growth, but often end up with a truncated gospel. If we are to live into the full counsel of God in the years to come, I believe we'll need a few experts in church shrink.

HIGH-OCTANE LEADERSHIP

A major part of our job as pastors of a large, growing church was to provide strong leadership. This comes with the territory of the seeker model. There were always new hills to be taken. With growing attendance came new challenges and opportunities. So we read about leadership. We attended conferences. We endeavored to be bigger leaders. We evaluated our staff based on the size of their leadership and the results they produced. We evaluated potential hires on their leadership capacity.

Obviously leadership is important in a church. This is not an argument for passivity or laziness. But the nonstop demands of the leadership cycle are costly. In the church, we are supposedly dealing with eternally significant issues, and yet the vision leaks and people forget. At times the leadership role requires us to say more than we believe, more passionately than we believe it. Occasionally the church needs to hear the speech from the pastor whether or not he or she feels like giving it. This role is a long way from the pastor as spiritual director. The truth is, we can't live every sermon or embody every value. The mission of the church is compelling, but not always. Ministry is sometimes a bore. Sin is sometimes attractive. We aren't always motivated. We aren't always at the top of our game. Our souls grow weary. We grow accustomed to running on fumes.

But the show must go on. So we get trapped in a role that requires us to be more than we are. We have no choice but to keep going even though the tank is empty. This damages the soul. We can be highly effective Christian leaders but marginal Christ followers. We can go years without a fresh encounter with God's love but still be effective communicators of the gospel. The demands of leadership can embitter us. The incessant complaints of religious consumers can plant seeds of sarcasm in our souls. Christian leadership is a dangerous business.

As our transition continued, we felt the fatigue of so many years of hard-driving leadership. We started to take our foot off the accelerator. The more we understood the gospel and the centrality of spiritual formation, the more we felt we had been sold a bill of goods about the church and about high-powered leadership. We were confused. Our angst quotient was rising. We had spent so much time and energy to build the church, and now we were questioning the leadership style we had adopted. We began to lose our edge as leaders. The church soon felt the vacuum of leadership.

Related to our unplugging from leadership was a growing question about the validity of the church. For years we had talked about it as the crucial player in God's plan for reaching the world. But now we were fleeing to the other end of the spectrum and began to question the institution. Did it really matter? Was it the hope of the world? Did it make any lasting difference in the lives of people? Was it worth saving? The angst put us on tilt.

For a couple of years we stopped attending to the organization. We didn't invest in our staff. We didn't start new ministries. We did the minimum to manage existing ones. We did not give vision talks. We allowed core values to sag. The lack of energy and constant brooding made people wonder if we were OK. We weren't. We were losing our resolve to lead because we weren't sure what we were leading was worth the effort.

A CHURCH OR A SECT?

Around this time an elder suggested that we let the church shrink to the committed two or three hundred. We would become a church for those who wanted to pursue the experiment of living in God's kingdom. For those who weren't interested, there were plenty of other churches in the area. We did not take this elder's suggestion lightly. We talked about whether this might be the path God had for us. The implications were extreme. But maybe this was God's calling.

A sect is composed of those who understand the requirements and expectations, and have agreed to live by them. Whether it's the Navy Seals, a monastic order or a football team, the participants know what they are signing up for and agree to abide by the code. Those who don't aren't allowed in or are forced out.

For nearly two years we grappled with the idea of Oak Hills becoming a sect of those who were committed to spiritual formation. Ultimately we decided that, by definition, the church is a community of people scattered across the spectrum of commitment. A few are hungry for transformation. Some are content to dabble. Most are in the middle. But the whole community makes up what we call "the church."

Jesus issues a high call to all those who are his followers. We take up our cross and follow him. It is daily death. We keep in step with God's Spirit. We engage in the challenging work of putting on the new self. We decrease so he can increase. We live in the name of Jesus. This is not a calling for the elite few. It is the normative way of apprenticeship to Jesus.

But in this world, reality rarely aligns with the ideal. The story of the Bible suggests the people of God are a community of unrefined, unfinished, conflict-loving, trouble-causing, sin-committing, cranky hypocrites. The bride is full of blemishes. The New Testament writers spend many words addressing the chasm between what we are called to be and what we actually are. The church includes the fully committed and the lukewarm. It is not a sect but an eclectic community of diverse people with varying degrees of commitment and interest in following Jesus and pursuing spiritual formation. Our hearts grow bigger for God by worshiping next to the guy who hates to sing, doesn't know the words and thinks the tune is lame. We are spiritually better off being in community with both the committed and the marginal.

ATTRACTIONAL OR MISSIONAL?

In our seeker days, the weekend service was the center of the Oak Hills universe. We thrived as an organization because this service was constantly funneling new people into the church. As the organization grew, so did the assimilation and support infrastructure. A kind of ecclesiastical narcissism set in.

The more we oriented the church around the gospel of the kingdom and spiritual formation, the more compelled we felt to send our people into this hurting world. Kent was instrumental in helping us think beyond the small story of organizational success and giving ourselves away to others. We needed to remember the world and minister to it with the resources of the kingdom. "Missional living" was a natural outcome of experiencing authentic transformation into Jesus.

We need to be incarnational. The world needs to *see* the good news. As we send people to their jobs, neighborhoods, schools and communities in the power of the kingdom of God, they bring the reality, power and goodness of the kingdom of God. "He wants us to

establish beachheads or bases of operation for the kingdom of God
wherever we are." We demonstrate a new and better Jesus way. The
church scattered with a mission is the hope of the world. Some of the
world will come to us. But we absolutely have to go to them.

We began to offer people service opportunities outside of our
church. We provided meals for a local ministry committed to serving
underprivileged families. We provided a monthly "For the Sake of
Others" brochure in our bulletin to inform our congregation of the
various serving opportunities available in our community. Being
missional was an outworking of being spiritually formed.

Reggie McNeal writes,

> The rise of the missional church is the single biggest develop-
> ment in Christianity since the Reformation. The post-Reforma-
> tion church of the modern era differed remarkably from its me-
> dieval predecessor. The missional church will just as dramatically
> distinguish itself from what we now call "church."

Equating the rise of the missional church with the Protestant Reformation is perhaps hyperbolic. But the missional emphasis provides
a much-needed corrective to a church-centered spirituality. We have
to move out and engage the world on its terms and turf. We have
business professionals, artists and football coaches who are passionate about meeting the needs of hurting people in our world. We have
had to work hard to make sure the church organization does not get
in the way of their desire to fulfill these good works. Our job as a
church is to challenge these people to live in the bigger story of what
God is doing in our community and around the world. These are
eternal concerns worthy of our time, money and talents. The church
is to be a locker room where people rally before going out and making
a difference by engaging in mission. Oak Hills doesn't need to devise
a program for every problem. Instead, we need to connect willing
servants with the needs.

But the missional movement also raises a concern. Perhaps this is
a misread on my part, but the missional movement seems to derive its

identity in deconstructing the established church. I heard a Christian leader casually suggest that churches should eliminate their programs because programs and strategies reinforce a skewed vision of what the church is and does. I understand the spirit of this. But it makes a giant leap toward turning the church into a sect of insiders who share the same values, believe the same truths and live them out the same way. Stripping a church of its programs would scare off the people in the congregation who are still in the process of exploring full apprenticeship to Jesus.

McNeal writes,

> Missional followers of Jesus don't belong to a church. They are the church. Wherever they are, the church is present. Church is not something outside of themselves that they go to or join or support; it is something they are. . . . The spiritual expression of Jesus followers was not characterized by a set of religious activities layered on top of other interests. Jesus invaded all areas of life. Church was not an event or a place; it was a way of life. It must become a way of life again. Enter the missional church.

Perhaps McNeal is trying to instigate change by hunkering down in an extreme position. But he does so at the risk of redefining the church as the community of those who "get it." It's much easier to be with people who get it. The hassle factor significantly drops; we don't have to convince; there's not as much conflict or disagreement. But again, the church is not a sect. It isn't a collection of people who see things the same way and have bought in at the same level. The church's events, programs and worship services are only one piece of a larger puzzle, but they *are* a piece. Obviously, they can become too important, so we need to find a rhythm. But we have to have a high theology of the *church gathered*. We have to believe in the mystery of what happens when God's people come together to worship, pray, receive the sacraments and love one another.

The either-or thinking is not helpful in resolving the complexity. Too often it seems as though missional ministries try to justify their existence with an attitude of "since the church hasn't done what it's suppose to do, we will." The church does need to move out into the world. It needs to repent of its narcissism. The church is God's people scattered and ministering to needs. But the church is also a place where the Christian story is repeatedly told. It is an event where we hear the story. It is a place where we worship with those who are pursuing life in God's kingdom and with those who are only marginally interested. It is a place we go to receive the sacraments. It is true that wherever God's people are, the church is present. But the building, facility or home where the church gathers is also a presence in a neighborhood. And its presence is a proclamation. We need the accountability of a larger community. We need an authority we willfully submit ourselves to. We are formed in ways we don't realize by being in the same worshiping community with people who don't like us and don't share our perspective or views. The diversity sharpens us and forms us in Jesus. A table at the local pub is a wonderful place to commune with others who trust and follow God. Good, formative things can happen there. But it's not the church. We tend to fill the pub table with our supporters, not our detractors; those who are like us, not those who are different. We need the local church.

Our journey has brought us full circle. In our seeker days we believed the church was the hope of the world. In the midst of our journey we lost that belief for a few years. But we have rediscovered a theology of the church that places a premium on the church gathered. In recent years we have been working to increase the level of ownership our people feel toward Oak Hills. We have been trying to increase the fun factor. We have been working to sharpen our values and goals. We have tried to devise a strategic plan that fits with our culture of spiritual formation. After a few years, we rehired our worship pastor who had resigned in the midst of our transition. He has helped bring energy and passion back into our weekend services. We believe in the local church. We believe participation in it is necessary for spiritual health. It is crucial to be accountable to others. It is crucial to live in submission to others. In spite of its many blemishes, the church is crucial in God's redemptive plan.

Shortly after our Donner Party experience, we had the privilege of spending time with Dallas Willard to discuss what was happening at Oak Hills. We asked what our church would look like at the end of this transition process. His answer was profound and prophetic. He told us the church would look much the same but would be completely different. We had no idea what he meant. But each year that passes, we understand a little more.

Churches have certain things to do. They have a presence in a town. They have regular services. They may have small groups. They may have various classes and programs for youth and children. They baptize. They celebrate Communion. They reach out to the hurting and forgotten. They host weddings and funerals. The outside may look the same. But when the church is driven by the transforming message of the good news, it is radically different.

Our understanding continues to morph. We are learning to live with the mystery and tension inherent in the church. Perhaps Bonhoeffer captured it best when he wrote to a friend during his first pastoral ministry:

> Should one not rejoice at a full church, or that people are coming who had not come for years, and on the other hand, who dare analyse this pleasure, and be quite certain that it is free from the seeds of darkness?

9

SPIRITUAL FORMATION

Do You Really Want to Be Healed?

MIKE LUEKEN

There exists in every person an unquenchable longing for God. Solomon said, "He has also set eternity in the human heart" (Ecclesiastes 3:11). We may be oblivious to this longing. Sometimes it hibernates beneath a host of diversions and distractions, noise and activity. The consuming grind of daily life deafens our ears to the eternity in our hearts.

But occasionally the longing becomes more acute. It may surface as a persistent ache, an afternoon daydream or a nagging question when the noise of life subsides. We hear a soul-stirring song, read a well-written paragraph, watch a poignant movie scene, revel in the beauty of creation or sample a slice of God-given pleasure, and for those few moments our longing is fulfilled. But as quickly as we taste satisfaction, it vanishes.

Fulfillment is elusive. When we think we have it cornered, it finds a way to escape. From an early age, we are trained to spend time and money seeking our longing's satisfaction—often in all the wrong places. It is a tragic quest. The longing is ultimately a desire for God. Maturity is realizing the longing remains unsatisfied on this side of eternity. The ache will not finally go away until we are with God. Still, we thirst for the One who made us and for the life he intended us to live.

LONGING FOR GOD

As I write this, I'm in a small dining area of a grocery store. There is a middle-aged woman staying connected to the world via her cell phone. A young mom is cramming a piece of coffeecake into her mouth and guzzling caffeine while trying to keep her small children out of trouble. A few tables away, a young couple eats bagels, drinks apple juice and exchanges flirtatious looks. I don't know any of these people. But I know something about them.

Each has a story that includes at least a few paragraphs on joy and a few others on pain. Through their unique experiences, relationships and choices, they have been spiritually formed. They may not believe in God or purpose to follow him, but who they are today is who they have trained themselves to be over the course of their life so far. Behind every dream, façade, pleasure pursuit, addiction, image-management strategy, busy schedule or all-consuming job, there is an unquenchable thirst for God. Our deepest longing is to experience God and be in relationship with him. This is the longing of every human soul—whether we know it or believe it.

The apostle Paul told the Colossians,

> For this reason, since the day we heard about you, we have not stopped praying for you. We continually ask God to fill you with the knowledge of his will through all the wisdom and understanding that the Spirit gives, so that you may live a life worthy of the Lord and please him in every way: bearing fruit in every good work, growing in the knowledge of God, being strengthened with all power according to his glorious might so that you may have great endurance and patience, and giving joyful thanks to the Father, who has qualified you to share in

the inheritance of his people in the kingdom of light. For he has rescued us from the dominion of darkness and brought us into the kingdom of the Son he loves, in whom we have redemption, the forgiveness of sins. (Colossians 1:9-14)

This passage reverberates with a call to spiritual formation. Paul prays the Colossians will have knowledge of God's will so they will live well, please God, bear fruit, endure hardship and joyfully give thanks. This is one of many biblical pictures of a person that the character of Jesus has been formed in. This formation naturally follows from the salvation God has accomplished through Christ. As we seek first the kingdom of God, our hearts are transformed. We become a new, Christlike person.

THE POSSIBILITY OF REAL CHANGE

Since the Donner experience, we have been enthralled with the possibility that human beings can actually change and become more like Jesus. We've oriented our church around this conviction. We have tried to take seriously Jesus' charge to "make disciples" (Matthew 28:19). As we apprentice under Jesus, by God's grace we can

Put to death the misdeeds of the body. (Romans 8:13)

Be made new in the attitude of your minds. (Ephesians 4:23)

Put on the new self, created to be like God in true righteousness and holiness. (Ephesians 4:24)

As Paul says, "We were therefore buried with him through baptism into death in order that, just as Christ was raised from the dead through the glory of the Father, we too may live a new life" (Romans 6:4). People increasingly immersed in the kingdom of God will experience an authentic heart-level change. They will gradually become new and better people. This is not an addendum to the gospel but a central tenet of it. This is not for the elite few who are interested but normative for all who put their trust in Jesus.

Much of our work over the past decade has been trying to instill hope for this new life into the culture of our church. Throughout the process, teaching has been a central and crucial means to accomplish this.

TEACHING

There is a fascinating story about Jesus healing a paralytic in John 5:1-9. Jesus saw this man lying by a pool and learned that he had suffered as an invalid for thirty-eight years, so Jesus asked him, "Do you want to get well?" (v. 6). At first glance, it's one of the few occasions where Jesus seemed to ask a dumb question; anyone with an affliction spanning nearly four decades would want relief, wouldn't they? However, Jesus knew that thirty-eight years of suffering could crush any hope of getting well, and perhaps more tragic, thirty-eight years could also paralyze the will to get well. The man on the mat knew his life didn't amount to much, but at least it was predictable. He was a tourist attraction of the temple, known as the one who suffered for thirty-eight years. Jesus was about to heal his body, which would forever change his identity.

This passage became a defining passage for our church and provided an overarching context for our teaching on spiritual formation—though we never set out searching for one. The question, "Do you want to be healed?" has become code language for "Do you want to be transformed?" This theme of transformation was woven into nearly all of our sermons soon after the Donner retreat. Regardless of the sermon topic, our message was essentially the same: cooperate with the Spirit of God to put off the old, put on the new and become the person Jesus redeemed you to be.

For example, the best thing we can do for our spouse and children is to cooperate with God to become a person who routinely and genuinely does good things. Similarly, we will win the battle with anger, lust, worry or control when we are retrained to choose the better way of Christ. With glaring redundancy we concluded our messages by encouraging people to spend unhurried time in solitude and silence, cultivating intimacy with Jesus. We were absolutely convinced spiritual formation in Christ was the key to living as God intended.

WE CAN'T ALWAYS GET WHAT WE WANT

As we continued to navigate the transition, we realized the strategy we had used to attract people to Oak Hills reinforced a self-preoccupation that ultimately hindered people's spiritual growth. They came because we gave them what they were looking for in a church, but in order for Christ to be formed in them, they needed to learn to subordinate their wants and needs. To make progress in the way of Christ, they had to die to self and its endless wants and preferences.

Getting what we want is part of daily life in our culture. Our satisfaction is paramount. If we don't like this television show, we hit the button. If we don't like this song on our iPod, we hit the button. If the church stops meeting our needs, we hit the button. Every day, we are told that what we have is insufficient. We are bombarded with messages to upgrade, trade in and borrow to buy. Our economy thrives on perpetual discontentment. The long-term consequence of this relentless marketing of dissatisfaction is that we become accustomed to having our needs met when and how we want. We become experts at "dissatisfaction remediation."

Ronald Rolheiser observes,

> Our lives become consumed with the idea that unless we somehow experience everything, travel everywhere, see everything, and are part of a large number of other people's experience, then our own lives are small and meaningless. We become impatient with every hunger, every ache, and every non-consummated area within our lives and we become convinced that unless every pleasure we yearn for is tasted, we will be unhappy. We stand before life too greedy, too full of expectations that cannot be realised, and unable to accept that, here, in this life all symphonies remain unfinished. When this happens an obsessive restlessness leaves us unable to rest or be satisfied because we are convinced that all lack, all tension, and all unfulfilled yearning is tragic. Thus, it becomes tragic to be alone; to be unmarried; to be married, but not completely fulfilled romantically

and sexually; to not be good-looking; or, be unhealthy, aged or handicapped. It becomes tragic to be caught up in duties and commitments which limit our freedom, tragic to be poor, tragic to go through life and not be able to taste every pleasure on earth and fulfill every potential inside us. When we are obsessed in this way it is hard to be contemplative. We are too focused on our own heartaches to be very open and receptive.

When this stark reality hit us, we faced a crossroads. We had to decide how to manage the tension between the message of self-denying discipleship and the reality of a congregation full of highly trained consumers. We could steadily push against the consumerism and hope to slowly win the battle, or we could assertively confront it. We chose the latter.

Perhaps our greatest lesson from the past decade is that it is spiritually formative to be dissatisfied and unable to resolve that dissatisfaction. In fact, there is hardly a better catalyst for transformation than to not get what we want. Sitting in the dissatisfaction, without frantically trying to resolve it, can do wonders for a human soul.

When we don't get what we want, we are more acutely aware of eternity. We are more apt to remember God. We learn what it really means to trust him. We remember the bigger story. When we don't get what we want, we have to deal with our inner restlessness. We have to face ourselves and our addictions. We have to deal with the various "medications" we use to cope with life. When we started these changes at Oak Hills, we put spiritual formation on the front burner, and the first thing that we saw that needed to be transformed was this raging desire to always get what we want.

THE UNWRITTEN CONTRACT

The combination of confronting consumerism, prioritizing spiritual formation and changing the feel of our weekend services broke an unwritten contract we had with our congregation. The contract was something like this: we provide people with programs and weekly services that satisfy their religious needs and preferences, and they continue to attend and support the church with their time and money. We do our part; they do their part.

We started teaching on the necessity of Christ being formed in our people, and we realized that some in our congregation never signed up for that. We discovered that people weren't necessarily coming to church to be formed in the image of Christ.

That's a sobering thought.

More sobering is the extent to which we had oriented the church around the concerns of those who were minimally interested in being apprentices of Jesus. This is not unique to larger churches like Oak Hills. The sad fact is, Christians don't always go to church to be transformed.

Paul prayed for the Philippians that their

> love may abound more and more in knowledge and depth of insight, so that you may be able to discern what is best and may be pure and blameless for the day of Christ, filled with the fruit of righteousness that comes through Jesus Christ—to the glory and praise of God. (Philippians 1:9-11)

Paul wanted them to grow toward fullness in Christ. We nod in agreement with Paul's words. We like his words. We like listening to sermons on his words. But at the end of the day, a good percentage of us don't really want to experience the reality depicted by these words. We like our lives just fine. They may need a touchup here or there, but nothing too radical, nothing too extreme.

We'd be better off if we just admitted it. It is sufficient for us that Jesus has forgiven our sins and secured our eternity, leaving our daily lives relatively unaffected. We are still the self-absorbed spouses we've always been. We continue to have a miser's heart. We use anger to overwhelm our opponents. We are trapped in lust. We manipulate and control to get what we want. We trust our political party more than Jesus. We ignore the poor. We have personal policies that are categorically opposed to the teaching of Christ. But we aren't bothered enough by these disconnects to put forth the effort to cooperate with the Holy Spirit because, in spite of what we claim, we really don't believe transformation is that important. It's good when it happens, and perhaps we should be more diligent at pursuing it, but it is not a natural or necessary consequence of salvation.

One man's story illustrates the split between salvation and transformation. We met over several weeks to discuss his struggling marriage. He is a long-time Christian and has been in church for much of his life. He is well-versed in the language of the Christian subculture. After hearing his story, it was obvious his marital system needed to be overhauled. They had fallen into a series of destructive ruts, and no amount of tweaking was going to help. Since I was talking to him, we focused on God's invitation to trust and follow in spite of his circumstances. We talked about what it would look like to choose a path of spiritual formation in this situation. The only thing he could control was who he was becoming. In spite of whatever else had to happen, for the marriage to get better, *he* was going to have to get better. There were specific issues in the relationship where he had been passive and complicit. Moving toward Christlikeness meant counter-intuitive action. He couldn't keep relating the same way and hope for a different result. It was time for him to make a holy mess. He needed to courageously wade into some long-overdue conflicts with his wife. He needed to initiate conversations about the marriage. But this pushed him beyond his comfort zone. He kept hesitating to make a move. Did he want to be healed? He was stuck.

Now he is a good man, a nice guy. This man loves God and does his best to follow Jesus. Obviously, there are situations and relationships in life that don't get fixed (and maybe can't get fixed). The fact was, his spiritual formation might not improve his marriage at all. It is, after all, a broken world. But the end result of the marriage was not the point. The tragedy is that this man has drifted along for many years as a "happy" and "nice" Christian, without realizing the gospel he believes invites him, indeed calls him, to transformation. He doesn't have to live with fear, passivity and complicity. Transformation is possible through the Spirit of the resurrected Christ.

Somewhere along the way, though, it became acceptable for this man—and many of us—to profess faith in Christ without signing up for being transformed. Perhaps this informs Dallas Willard's remarks:

> The primary mission field for the Great Commission today is made up of the churches in Europe and North America. That is where the Great Disparity is most visible, and from where it threatens to spread to the rest of the world. . . .
>
> So the greatest issue facing the world today, with all its heart-breaking needs, is whether those who, by profession or culture, are identified as "Christians" will become *disciples*—students, apprentices, practitioners—*of Jesus Christ*, steadily learning from him how to live the life of the Kingdom of the Heavens into every corner of human existence.

ALTERNATIVES TO GENUINE SPIRITUAL FORMATION

In our efforts to orient the church around spiritual formation, we discovered how tempting it is for people to settle for a cheap alternative rather than the real thing. Some of us are consoled by the fact that, while we may not be experiencing transformation, at least we are frustrated by our complacency. We are satisfied with our spiritual dissatisfaction. We may be dealing with the same sin issue we were a decade ago but at least we are frustrated about it. We may even like the impression others have of us as being frustrated by our lack of spiritual maturity. If we can't actually change, we can at least relish the fact that people think of us as wanting to change. We settle for impressing a few people. As C. S. Lewis said, "We are far too easily pleased." As Jesus put it, we have "received [our] reward in full" (Matthew 6:5).

Some people equate spiritual formation with trying hard to be good. It is true that transformation is hard work. It takes time and effort. But it's actually easier to try hard to change outward behaviors and touch up the exterior of our lives. It's easier and more tempting to reduce spiritual formation to legalistic adherence to a list of rules. Our righteousness should "[surpass] that of the Pharisees and the teachers of the law" (Matthew 5:20). But we must do more than try really hard. Our hearts must become more like Jesus so that we instinctively want what he wants and routinely do what he would do.

Others think the way to transformation is to work through a series of spiritual formation classes or programs. These can be helpful tools, but completing them is no guarantee we are closer to transformation. The Bible is a vital means of growth, but in-depth Bible studies often stifle the growth. We study to conquer, not to be changed. We dig deeper into the Bible to sharpen our understanding of its content and meaning, not to have it sharpen us. We must constantly be reminded that spiritual formation is not about learning more information.

THE CRUCIAL MATTER OF INTENTION

Much of what we learned through our church's transition—and what we are still learning—has to do with the role of intention in the formation journey. We've seen this surface countless times through the years. We won't grow in Christ unless we decide we want to.

The Holy Spirit is obviously the primary agent of spiritual transformation. "Since we live by the Spirit, let us keep in step with the Spirit" (Galatians 5:25). He can accomplish what he wants in a person through a variety of means. He is in charge of the process. He makes transformation happen. But he will not overpower us to get it done. We have to want it. Our will has to intend to put on the character of Christ. We have to put forth effort in order to realize the new life Jesus has for us.

Intention is the forgotten issue in the spiritual formation conversation. We routinely talk about God's desire that we would put off the old self and put on the new. We talk about the various spiritual disciplines we can practice to create space for God in our hearts. But we don't talk as much about our will or our intention. The Holy Spirit will never usurp our will. If we don't want Christ formed in us, then not even the Spirit will make it happen. Our passivity in our spiritual growth is a hangover from the Reformation. We are afraid of turning grace into works. So instead, we turn grace into a divine magic that does everything for us. But to experience spiritual formation in Christ, we have to want Christ formed in us. This has nothing to do with earning God's favor; it has to do with how we respond to the undeserved grace of God.

One man came to me because he was becoming increasingly aware of a growing problem with anger. He saw it erupt in flash moments. He saw it creeping into his attitude toward his wife. He heard himself explode at his kids. So we started meeting regularly and exploring the story of his anger. After several meetings and much talking, it was time to ramp up to a new level. I suggested an assignment of keeping a journal in which he made note of the circumstances surrounding his surges of anger. What had happened? What was going through his mind? Was he in a hurry? Had he gotten enough sleep? Were there similarities between the various situations? It was hard work. He commented more than once on how draining it was to pay this much attention to the state of his own heart. He was beginning to understand the crucial role of intention in the spiritual life.

FOUNDATIONS OF SPIRITUAL FORMATION

We concluded one weekend service by asking people to consider what God might want them to surrender. We invited people to come forward and release whatever they sensed he wanted from them. The response was significant. After the service, I saw one of our elders sitting alone near the front of the room. He'd been a Christian his whole life and carried Oak Hills in his heart since it began. He came forward because he sensed God urging him to surrender his Christianity. He felt he needed to repent of his nominal evangelical Christianity so he could embrace life in God's kingdom. I knew what he meant, but it was staggering to hear him say it.

He was a solid Christian who loved God and sought to order his life around Jesus. But something was missing. He wasn't being transformed in any authentic way. He wasn't trusting God with any radical edge. But now he was wanting to live out the gospel of the kingdom. He was especially intrigued to bring his business under the reign of

God. He starting making specific business decisions in an attempt to be more kingdom centered. He became a shining example of someone who took seriously Jesus' call to apprenticeship. He has genuinely changed over the last several years as he has reoriented his life and business around the principles of the kingdom of God.

We've found through the years of our transition that there are many people like this in our church who are hungry for a deeper life with God. They want to see him working actively in their lives. They want to learn to live in his presence throughout the day. They want the routines of life to become a burning bush where they meet and experience God. They don't want to be weird. They don't want to *pretend* they are different. They actually intend to *be* different and have taken radical steps along the way. Our many interactions with these people over the last decade have helped us identify four foundational aspects of the spiritual formation process.

First, transformation happens in the specific details of our hearts and lives. For many, one of the first hurdles to overcome is the sheer size of the spiritual formation mountain. It is overwhelming to consider the magnitude of what needs to change in our lives. There are so many unformed areas, we don't know where to start. Generalities are a good hiding place. "Jesus died for my sins" is less scandalous than "Jesus died for my out-of-control anger that severely damages the people I love the most." "I'm a sinner" is easier to admit than "I'm a lustaholic." In generalities, no one is exposed. But no one really grows. Real transformation happens in the unattractive details of our lives.

Paul writes:

> It is God's will that you should be sanctified: that you should avoid sexual immorality; that each of you should learn to control your own body in a way that is holy and honorable, not in passionate lust like the pagans, who do not know God; and that in this matter no one should wrong or take advantage of a brother or sister. The Lord will punish all those who commit such sins,

as we told you and warned you before. For God did not call us to
be impure, but to live a holy life. (1 Thessalonians 4:3-7)

Paul urges his readers toward spiritual formation in a specific area.
He wades into the uncomfortable details of sexual sin and casts a vision of the kingdom to those drowning in sexual impurity.

The formation of our hearts and souls happens when we choose to
walk into the messy details. The process of spiritual formation is in-
vasive. The Word of God divides "soul and spirit, joints and marrow"
(Hebrews 4:12). The Spirit of God honors our willingness. He meets
us as we step out in faith. He works in specific issues and areas of our
lives to bring a new vision into reality.

*Second, to retrain our hearts and minds, we must take counter-
intuitive action.* As we start considering the details of our lives that
need transformation, we begin seeing how automatic our responses
are. We don't have to try very hard to get angry at the driver who cuts
us off. Our anger comes easily and routinely because of our many
years of training in it. When the circumstances arise, anger is ready.
Traditional disciplines like solitude and silence, prayer and Scripture
reading can help renovate our hearts and root out the anger. These
are vital to experiencing lasting change.

But in addition, one of the most commonly prescribed spiritual
disciplines at Oak Hills is, "Do the opposite of what you want to do
or feel like doing." The controlling person has to put themselves in
situations where someone else calls the shots. The self-absorbed
person has to shut their pie hole and listen. The isolated loner needs
relationships. The socialite needs solitude. The person drowning in
shame needs to show up. The angry person needs to underreact.

Perhaps this sounds like spiritual formation by trying hard to be
different. It's actually a discipline to help us retrain our whole being
in the way of Christ. It's an intensely practical way to start cultivating
a new heart out of which new things can flow. Counterintuitive action thrusts us beyond the borders of our comfort zones and into
unfamiliar territory where we are more dependent on God.

Third, identity is usually a core issue in the spiritual formation process. Our issues and conditions have a way of leaking into our identity and becoming part of who we are. We forge a bond with our dark side. We hate our sins, but we also love them. We want freedom from our struggles, but we want to hold onto them. We can't live another day with them, but we can't imagine life without them. Fits of anger provide us with a few moments of freedom where we can finally be unedited without concern for what others think. When we blow up in anger we usually get what we want. Lust offers sexual satisfaction without the hassle of intimacy. Shame justifies our lack of showing up in relationships and confirms our instincts to hide. Busyness makes us feel necessary and important. Worry sustains our false sense of control. Lying keeps our true self in the shadows.

Spiritual formation into Jesus' likeness is liberation from sin conditions, but who will we be after we are changed? What will life be like without anger or lust or fear or control? The uncertainty solidifies us as a dabbler in Christian discipleship. Thirty-eight years of anything sets us into a way of thinking and living that will not be easy to undo. We settle for accepting Jesus and waiting for heaven, but not much changes today. So Jesus' question to the invalid is his question to us: Do we want to get well?

Because so many people struggle with identity, we designed a curriculum to help people unpack their own life stories, hoping they will discover God's gracious hand on them even through dark times. We have found that there is freedom in facing our pasts with courage and with confidence in God to help us move forward.

Fourth, personal transformation has implications far beyond the individual. One man in our church decided some years ago that he wanted to deal with the anger in his heart. He was tired of the outbursts. He was tired of screaming at drivers he didn't know. He was tired of blowing up at the people he loved. He sought the help of a community of men. He confessed his sin to trusted advisers. He spent several years digging at the roots of his anger with the help of friends and counselors. He incorporated a few spiritual disciplines into his life to cultivate a new heart. In time, God brought change. His anger subsided. He wasn't as quick to overreact. He was learning patience. The people near him noticed.

But as he experienced God's transforming work, his family had to adjust to this new person. For as long as his wife and children could remember, their husband or dad was angry. They had learned to relate to him as an angry guy. They lived this drama for years. In ways they weren't even aware of, they adjusted to his anger and learned how to live with it.

But his transformation changed their system. He was not playing the role the family was used to. His wife started realizing she'd been able to ignore her own "stuff" because his anger was the prevailing issue in their marriage. It kept her from having to face herself. His transformation sent her into a bit of a tailspin. There were times when she tried to push his buttons in the hope that he would return to his old self. The couple discovered there were unresolved marital issues that had been kept hidden by the big issue of his explosive anger. In turn, the children realized the drama of dad's anger trained them in how to function in chaos, and they began to notice that they were more at ease in a tumultuous environment.

"ONE THING" GROUPS

Talking about spiritual formation and teaching on it are not sufficient to instill it into the DNA of the church. Eventually, our people wanted hands-on, practical ways to pursue the life Jesus was inviting them to live. The prevailing question was "Now what? What can we do to experience this good life Jesus offers?"

For many years we had a strong system of small groups to help people connect into the life of the church and grow in their faith. As we continued orienting around spiritual formation, community became even more crucial. In fact, the delivery system for bringing this emphasis on spiritual formation into a church has to be through smaller communities that are intentional about it. The formational journey is not a solo flight. We need others to encourage and challenge us along the way. But the drift in most small groups is away from intentional spiritual formation. They become "Bible studies." Or they become social gatherings. They gradually cease to be groups that are oriented around the singular goal of spiritual formation in Christlikeness.

So one of the first practical ideas we brought to our congregation was "one thing" groups. The purpose of these groups was to help people intentionally pursue spiritual formation in one specific area. God has reasonable expectations for us. He understands we are made of dust. We can't hurry the formation process. It was liberating for people to have permission to focus on one area and essentially forget the rest. The mountain became smaller. It made the journey more manageable and doable. Obviously, by intentionally pursuing growth in one area we are actually growing in many areas because our hearts are changing.

One of the challenges was to bring leaders onboard and help them see themselves as catalysts for spiritual growth in the lives of those they are leading. As the "pastors" of these groups, they needed to be trained in how to gently lead a person to a spiritually formative discovery. They needed to learn how to ask redemptively disruptive questions. They needed to know how to dig into the soul. They needed to be excellent listeners. Most of all, the leaders needed to value intentionality so the groups continued to make progress in the new life of Jesus.

Groups of three to six would spend a year together identifying their "one thing" and pursuing the necessary disciplines, experiences, knowledge or relationships that have catalyzed spiritual growth—both in the Bible and throughout history. The process begins by spending unhurried time with God and having an attentive heart to identify the "one thing" God wants to transform in us. We use the Sermon on the Mount as a guide. People choose things like anger, lust, worry, control, patience, joy, love and gentleness. These groups are crucial in our church's journey toward spiritual formation. We started to move beyond sermons and into the practical ways by which a person actually becomes more like Jesus.

There were about one hundred people in the twenty "one thing" groups we started. Each person spent a month or so attending to their one thing. They noticed when it surfaced. They paid attention to the circumstances surrounding its emergence. They talked about what was happening in their hearts surrounding their "one thing." Conversations revolved around the ongoing clarification of the one thing and where its roots were in the person's life. Repeatedly people experienced what we called "the trap-door phenomena." They would identify one thing and attend to it for a while—only to step on a trap door that dropped them down to an even deeper issue. Their initial "one thing" was often a doorway to the discovery of an even bigger, more pressing root issue.

Many found that this process of identifying an area needing growth—and then purposefully attending to it—jump-started their journey of spiritual formation. As people gained clarity on where God wanted to move in them, they began orienting their lives around a handful of formational practices and experiences that would invite God's transforming power. They constructed a realistic rule of life to give them direction. They started practicing unceasing prayer. They memorized Scripture. They spent time in solitude. Throughout the process, people confessed, prayed and shared the journey with one another.

Spiritual formation wasn't a theory any more. People knew what they could "do." Some were profoundly changed through this experience. Others were minimally impacted. But we gained valuable insight into the process of spiritual formation through the experiment of these groups.

One group spent several months identifying their various one things. They worked on their spiritual formation plan, discussing and revising it in their weekly meetings. They met for about eighteen months, and at one point, the group had a gut-check conversation. They were discussing where they were heading as a group and what was next. The conversation turned toward their intention to change. Did they really want to put forth this effort? Did they want to be healed? A couple of people in the group opened up and admitted they didn't really want to change. They knew they should want transformation, but they didn't. The hassle of walking into the interior chaos was too costly. They were content to stay where they were. It was sad at one level, but at least it was refreshingly honest.

These days we are seeking to create a culture where leaders who are passionate about spiritual formation are unleashed to experiment and use their creativity to figure out how to foster intentional formation communities.

RETREATS

One of the most helpful tools we implemented was our weekend spiritual-formation retreats. In addition to having a teaching component, these retreats were highly experiential. Initially, we structured the retreat around one or two spiritual disciplines, like solitude and silence or worship and prayer. Groups of thirty or so would spend a weekend together at a local convent or monastery for instruction and practice of these disciplines. Kent and I would lead these retreats along with some skilled laypeople who were seasoned practitioners of the spiritual disciplines. The retreats continued to broaden the spiritual formation conversation, but they also helped people get down into the specific details of their hearts, minds and bodies that needed transformation. We learned about the impact of hurry on the human soul when we started the retreat with four hours of solitude—and found out later that half of the group spent most of the time sound asleep! Their bodies were ravished by their ruthless commitment to hurry.

We also conducted retreats on the various issues raised in the Sermon on the Mount. We promoted these retreats as opportunities to learn how to live without anger, lust, worry and so forth. We spent a weekend exploring anger and its roots and tentacles, and we talked about how to rid our hearts of it. People struggle with the audacious claim that we can live without anger, but that is what we kept stressing. Whatever we can accomplish with anger can be accomplished better without it. These retreats were another practical way for people to exercise their intention in spiritual formation.

A few years ago we organized our formation retreats into a two-year experience we call "the spiritual formation academy." Each year consists of four stay-at-home weekend retreats on our campus. The first year focuses on the kingdom of God, the importance of intention and a careful look at six spiritual disciplines. In between the retreats, we hold huddle gatherings for people to process the reading and the exercises they are doing. The second year attempts to turn people out toward the world to see the needs of those around us. It has been an experiment in moving beyond individual formation toward formation in community. As we continue to learn and experiment, we anticipate more groups that structure themselves around the singular pursuit of formation in Christ.

THE PASTOR AS SPIRITUAL DIRECTOR

As helpful as the curriculum, groups, retreats and academy were in our situation, it is not possible to mass-produce transformation through a one-size-fits-all program. Spiritual formation is inherently inefficient because each person has a different road to travel. There are too many unique factors in each person's life to standardize the process. Their upbringing, pain, past religious experiences, personality and sin tendencies affect their journey toward healing. This is why it is so important for pastors to rediscover their calling as spiritual directors. Herding people through a series of classes or curriculum without careful regard for their individual stories hinders spiritual growth. Completing another class might give those of us in church leadership a sense of accomplishment, but transformation is not like making widgets. Spiritual formation is a relational endeavor requiring individual pastoral direction and care. This may seem inefficient, and indeed, it puts formation at odds with the strategic nature of many larger churches.

I recently had a conversation with a woman in our church who has been with us throughout our journey. We were talking about her experience in the spiritual formation academy and the various things

God has done in her life in recent years. She talked about coming to a point in her life a few years ago when "it wasn't working." Life, relationships and Christianity were not working. She began exploring other religions, searching for answers. It occurred to her that Jesus was there, ready and willing to be her mentor. Perhaps the time had come to seek him more purposefully. She became intentional in her pursuit of God and life in his kingdom. She joined the spiritual formation academy. She vowed she was going to fully participate in the experience. She would ask questions. She would do the work. She would struggle with the material. She would do the disciplines. All of this was against her instincts. Her default was to hide in the shadows and strive for invisibility, but instinctively she knew that adopting that same strategy would produce the same disappointing results.

I listened to her describe her journey. My mouth stayed shut. While she was talking, the thought occurred to me, *This is why we do this. This is the point. This is what we vaguely hoped for ten years ago.*

We continue to learn what apprenticeship to Jesus looks like and how transformation actually happens. We want to be a church that helps hungry people make real progress in their spiritual formation. Obviously, not everyone is interested, but the years of staying at this have produced a hunger in many to see themselves formed in Christ. When the church is training people to be apprentices of Jesus and turning them loose into a dying world, we are fulfilling the Great Commission. And there is no work on the planet more exhilarating than that!

10

OUTREACH

A Burning Passion for the World

MIKE LUEKEN

ℰ

*W*hen I first became a Christian I had a one-track mind to introduce others to Jesus. I wanted them to know him. I wasn't always tactful in the process, but I had a white-hot passion for evangelism. I had found life's answer, and I wanted everyone to know about it. Perhaps the passion was fueled by youthful idealism. Maybe this is what happens on the faith "honeymoon," but it can't be sustained. Or maybe we are just really skilled at making excuses so we feel better. Perhaps the real issue is that we gradually lose our passion for those outside of God's family because we grow attached to the world, and we don't believe people are in that much trouble without Jesus.

This chapter is the hardest for me to write. The edge and attitude I have around this subject is self-directed. Even when I was assertively sharing my faith, I never thought of myself as an effective evangelist. I don't like how I avoid evangelism. I don't like my lack of boldness.

This chapter is also difficult because at Oak Hills we have struggled with how to do outreach and evangelism in a manner that is consistent with our understanding of the gospel and our theology of the church. We've considered many hard, complicated questions. We have not discovered many answers. Mostly, we've been confused. Our confusion has left us paralyzed. Evangelism is the weakest part of our church.

THE EARLY MISSION
In our seeker years outreach was our strength. Our mission was to reach nonchurched people. This was our rallying point. It was our unifying cause. Lost people mattered to God, and we were passionate about reaching them. We had embraced Willow Creek's seven-step strategy to help people know their part in the process. People were intentionally building relationships with lost people and inviting them to church. Stories were constantly being told of how God was changing lives.

There were other factors that made this strategy effective. We were located in one of the fastest-growing communities in the Sacramento region. New people were moving into town each month. We were the only church in the area aggressively pursuing the seeker-targeted strategy. Our people were excited to be part of something fresh and creative. Nonchurched people were intrigued. The attendance kept growing. Lives were being impacted. Our passion for lost people was the strength of the church.

When spiritual formation became the priority, we started seeing some blind spots. While the seeker service helped our congregation think beyond themselves and was an effective way to get people in the front door, it artificially propped up the value of evangelism. Our passion for reaching the lost was clouded by the excitement and adrenaline of being involved in a rapidly growing church. We loved the lost, but we also loved the success we felt when another new person started attending. The value was also propped up because inviting someone to a weekend service became synonymous with personal evangelism. As important as it is to bring a friend to church, it does not replace the slow, hard work of building relationships with the lost, engaging them in spiritual conversations and sharing the good news with them.

We also began to realize that the method of the seeker strategy did not support our understanding of the gospel as an invitation to a new way of living. In fact, the method got in the way. The seeker approach put a premium on an individual's anonymity. But this was at odds with our conviction that the gospel was a new life lived in community with others. We needed to be known if we had any hope of spiritual formation. In addition, at the end of our seeker service we often invited people to make a decision to follow Jesus. Many responded. And though we encouraged discipleship, it wasn't a central concern. Evangelism was about making a decision to be a Christ follower. That was the most important step. Discipleship was about learning how to actually follow Jesus. That was more of an optional step. We had separated evangelism and discipleship. Of course we encouraged people to grow in their relationship with Jesus. We had a variety of ministries and programs designed to develop disciples (small groups, midweek New Community services, serving opportunities). We continuously reminded people that there was more. But discipleship was for "those who were interested." It was not central to our invitation or to the individual's decision to follow Jesus.

The Donner retreat provided a needed corrective. We had spent many years reaching out and inviting other people, but now we were trying to slow down and pay attention to the specific formational issues in our own hearts and lives. We had inspired our church to care for the lost, but now we were stressing the importance of becoming more like Jesus by taking on his character. We had been known for our innovative and creative weekend service aimed at nonchurched people, but now we were introducing programs and experiences designed to dig into the details of our heart and unearth core issues that needed to be transformed. In a relatively short period of time the pendulum swung from Oak Hills being rigorously evangelistic to almost exclusively inward. Again, in our situation we needed a correction. But as we transitioned toward more of an emphasis on spiritual formation, we went too far. We forgot a crucial component of holistic spiritual formation. We forgot about the world. We forgot God's heart for lost people. We lost the passion for evangelism.

FINDING THE FLOW

A decade has elapsed since we began reorienting our church. Our town has dramatically changed in the last decade. The population growth has slowed significantly. New churches have emerged. More people than ever are skeptical of organized religion. The percentage of nonchurched people continues to rise. It's a different cultural climate than it was in the 1990s.

Much of our effort these past several years has been spent sorting through the theological and conceptual evangelistic issues in light of our understanding of the gospel as an invitation to live in God's kingdom. We have not developed profound new methods for reaching this culture. We've struggled with the practical challenges of how to share the good news with a hurting world in a way that reinforces the gospel as new life, not just forgiveness of sins and heaven after death. We have mostly grappled with hard, confusing questions. How do we evangelize people into a life of apprenticeship to Jesus? How do we evangelize without being concerned with the numerical growth of the church? How do we invite people into the community of faith without getting caught up in whether or not they are coming to our church? How do we contextualize the language of the kingdom so people understand what it means? Is it even possible to devise an authentic strategy for evangelism that reinforces our understanding of the gospel?

Over the years of our existence, we have at times truncated the notion of evangelism. It was about inviting people to church more than inviting them to be apprentices of Jesus. Since we've changed direction, we've been guilty of focusing on discipleship and ignoring the evangelistic call. We were more concerned with growing in Christ, not reaching the lost. So one of the most important lessons we've learned is to maintain the interconnectedness between spiritual formation, mission and evangelism. They flow in and out of each other. We need to keep a rhythm between cultivating the inward life (spiritual formation) and giving ourselves away in outward service (mission and evangelism). When formation, mission and evangelism become independent departments, they drift toward legalistic obligation, become the hobbyhorse of an elite few and lose their momentum.

So we spend time alone in solitude and silence. We study the Scriptures and pray. We attend to the formational issues in our heart and life. We move out and engage the world. We pour ourselves out in service. We care for the world's needs. We introduce others to the Savior. We stay nourished by practicing solitude, prayer, worship, fasting, community, Scripture reading and other disciplines. Intentional apprenticeship leads to mission and evangelism. Mission and evangelism compels us to intentional apprenticeship.

LIVING THE GOSPEL

There is a man who has been at Oak Hills since the church started. He has served faithfully over the years and is an avid supporter of the ministry. During the seeker years he regularly brought people to church and had stories to tell of God's work in their life. A few years after we changed direction, he asked an important question: "What's the strategy? Tell me what I am supposed to go out in the world and do." He illustrated how far we had swung. Not too many years earlier our strategy for reaching people was crystal clear. Our people knew exactly what they were supposed to do. But now many were asking a similar question as this guy. They didn't know how to bring the gospel to their friends. We didn't have much of an answer.

Whenever we tried to answer the how-to question, we ended up stressing the priority of living out the message of the kingdom. This simply cannot be presumed; nor can its importance be overstated. It's so basic it feels like a cop-out. But we discovered that the most important strategy for reaching lost people is Christians living Christianly. Effective evangelism starts by cooperating with God to become a new kind of person out of whom new and better things routinely and easily flow.

Scores of people profess to be Christian, and yet the statistics of our communities do not improve. The percentage of nonchurched people continues to rise. Anger and sexual distortion dominate the headlines. Charitable giving by Christ followers is pathetic. Survey after survey confirms that the priorities and values of professing Christians mirror those of society in general. Yet Jesus said we are salt and light (Matthew 5:13-14).

If the gospel is an invitation to a new way of living, then to be credible witnesses we have to be experiencing this new life at some level. There has to be a compelling and attractive difference in how we live. It may not be a difference that is detectable in surveys about Christian behavior. Perhaps it is more qualitative. Maybe it is a difference others sense rather than see. But if Jesus is who he claims to be, and we are his followers, it stands to reason that we should be living a new kind of life. In the early years of our transition we dedicated ourselves to continuously emphasizing who we are and how we are living as the key component of our witness in the world.

We will not share what we do not have. It is hard to sustain our motivation to witness to the richness of life in God's kingdom when we are not living in it and seeing the difference it makes. This is why it is much easier to invite people to church than to apprenticeship. If we continue to succumb to anger, lust, worry and fear, our talk of new life is empty rhetoric. Our evangelistic fervor is fueled by fresh encounters with the love and presence of God, which produce the fruit of a changed heart. As we experience transformation in the details of our lives, we will be more inclined to share the new life with others.

For the last four years, I've had the opportunity to coach football at one of the local high schools. So for several months of the year, I've interacted with other coaches, young men and their parents, many of whom are not Christ followers. This has thrust me beyond the walls of my office and the church campus, and into the middle of the real world. Not once have I shared the gospel in any structured or formal way. But my presence has opened numerous conversations about life, faith and character. The simple notion of being sent to live differently has been a central component of our message to our church.

STOKING THE FIRE

Once we eliminated the weekend seeker service, we were without a regular evangelistic event in the life of our church. As artificial as it may have been, that service kept our people thinking about their lost friends. We found that after a few years focused on spiritual formation, people's passion for evangelism diminished. The challenge we have faced for several years is how to relight the fire. We've seen how the hurried busyness makes it extremely hard for people to have the time or the space to even care about their lost friends.

Michael Green notes,

> One of the most notable impressions the literature of the first and second century made upon me as I wrote this book was the sheer passion of these early Christians. They were passionately convinced of the truth of the gospel. They were persuaded that men and women were lost without it. It was the key to eternal life, without which they would perish. They shared in God's own love, poured out on a needy world. They paid heed to Christ's Great Commission. They sought to interpenetrate society with the gospel which had had so profound an effect upon them. Christianity for them was no hour's slot on a Sunday. It affected everything they did and everyone they met. As far as we can tell, their church life was warm and nourishing for the most part, and equipped people to move out with the good news. The ordinary Christians, the missionaries, the academics, the women, all seem to have shared in this same passionate commitment to the cause. . . . Not until we in the West burn with a passion which is almost a pain to reach people with the gospel will they be likely to take the matter seriously.

Green's description of the bristling passion of the early Christians makes me stop to consider my own fire for the gospel. Am I passionately convinced of its truth? Am I convinced people are destined to perish without it? There are unreflective answers to these questions, and then there is the sobering truth.

We've asked our church many times: Do we really believe the gospel is good news about life today? Do we believe people outside God's family are missing anything? Related to this is the question of need. People living in suburban America are not typically facing urgent needs that they cannot resolve with their own resources. So we've asked: How do we reach people who do not think they have any needs? What does the gospel offer the comfortable suburbanite who is not actively searching for anything?

Not long ago a team from our church went to Cambodia for a two-week missions plunge. They spent time in towns and villages known for their brothels and for the sexual exploitation of teenage girls. A member of the team told me about a local pastor in one of the towns who spends one to two hours a day walking the streets and praying for his community.

I drive by quaint subdivisions in our community every day on my way to the office. I've never once wandered their streets praying for the hundreds of people who live there. Why? It could be because I'm lazy. Maybe, in spite of what I say, I don't really care about them. Maybe I think they are hopeless idolaters who have embraced the materialism of suburbia. Maybe I love the poor and marginalized, but I have contempt for the relatively rich. Perhaps I am trapped in a cycle of soul-damaging judgment. Maybe I'm a desperate hypocrite who is similarly stuck in the suburban ghetto but I see myself as exempt from its dangers. Whatever the reason, I'm sure I do not have Jesus' heart for these "neighbors." But if I did, would they listen? It's one thing to walk streets lined with brothels and corruption and sexual deviants. The need is obvious. It's not so obvious on streets with four-bedroom homes, plush green lawns and three-car garages.

As previously mentioned, we have been slow to discover viable ways of sharing our faith in a manner consistent with spiritual formation. But we have found a few practical means.

Prayer walks. We live at such a frantic pace that we stop noticing the actual people in the communities where we live. We found that a good old-fashioned prayer walk was a great help at slowing us down and helping us "see" our neighbors as people who need God. There is something powerful about walking the streets where we live and praying for God to work in our hearts and in the lives of those who live in these neighborhoods. Perhaps the praying helps deconstruct the façade of a well-manicured lawn and nice house. The prayer walk also reduces the artificiality of suburbia. It reminds us that no matter how perfect things may look on the outside, people still need God.

Service. Robert Mulholland defines spiritual formation as "a process of being conformed to the image of Christ for the sake of others." It took us a while, but eventually we learned that the "for the sake of others" piece is essential to understanding the broader purpose of spiritual formation. Discipleship produces hospitality to a hurting world. Discipleship inspires sacrificial service. Discipleship spurs love for lost people.

We got stuck in navel-gazing mode for a few years. But eventually we saw the connection between spiritual formation and outreach. We began to more purposefully care for the marginalized. We'd always had compassion ministries and had been active in crosscultural missions. But the more we pursued spiritual formation, the more we were convinced that Christlike people intentionally reach out to those who are ignored, forgotten and marginalized. They are our neighbors we are called to welcome and love. We make room for them. We share what we have with them. We give ourselves away in service to them. We meet their practical needs with no strings attached. We don't do this to convert them. We don't do it with an ulterior motive or agenda. We aren't ministering to impress them with our benevolence, hoping that they will attend our church. We reach out to the lonely, the forgotten, the poor and the marginalized with no strings attached because this is what Jesus did.

This is not novel to the Christian church. Benevolent mercy efforts are becoming increasingly common. People are realizing fulfillment is found in sacrifice. We have come to believe that an effective way to evangelize the lost is to invite them to serve alongside of us in these mercy ministries.

Staff. We dedicated a staff person to lead us in outreach. She made contacts with local and international compassion ministries. She helped bridge the gap between our intention and action. Our church is located in the heart of suburbia, with all its dangers and threats. The vast majority of the people in our community are middle to upper class. It takes sustained vision and energy to rally comfortable people to care for the marginalized. It's much easier to ignore them. But the steady, consistent work has been fruitful. Our people are more aware of what God is doing beyond the walls of our church. They care more about the world. Reggie McNeal defines missional living as "seeing all life as a way to be engaged with the mission of God in the world." All life is an opportunity to bring God's grace and power to a world in need. We still have work to do, but today we are more of a "missional" church. More people are participating in God's grander mission of reconciliation and restoration.

Arts events. Oak Hills supports the personal evangelism efforts of our people through a handful of seeker-friendly events that happen each year. One of these is an evening with the arts, which we call Mosaic. We do our best to provide quality music, drama, dance and other creative elements around a theme relevant to lost people. Initially, we encouraged our congregation to invite their friends to this event. More recently, we have turned Mosaic into a benefit for a local underresourced school or program or ministry to those in need. Inviting non-Christians to join in seeking to alleviate the needs of a hurting world is a practical means of introducing people to Christ.

Finding the words. In our context we have primarily emphasized the importance of demonstrating the good news of God's kingdom. It shows people what we believe. And there is a time to demonstrate the kingdom. But we've also seen our church lose its nerve when it comes to boldly talking with non-Christians about the gospel and life under

God. Henry H. Knight III and F. Douglas Powe Jr. write, "The risk of proclaiming God's word is at the heart of evangelism. God works in all of our lives and we are called to testify to others about God's actions." The world needs to see the gospel. But sometimes words are necessary. Sometimes people need to hear the gospel courageously proclaimed. Effective evangelism is both demonstration and proclamation.

It's really hard to teach boldness. Our sense is that people who are genuinely experiencing the goodness of life in Christ will easily and routinely share their faith with others. Even so, we found that people need training to know what to say when the opportunity arises. There is no shortage of tools available to help people share their faith with seekers. But people are not responsive to formulaic presentations. They are looking for something real.

As our understanding of the gospel changed, we found a shortage of tools that helped our people share the good news about life in God's kingdom. So we have offered our people a how-to training class that helps them share the gospel of the kingdom. Our primary point is that sharing our faith must occur in the context of a relationship built with our seeking friends. Usually, they have to see our faith reflected in the newness of our life before they will allow us to share with them.

An alternative community. A harmful side effect of our seeker strategy was that in the process of trying to identify with our suburban culture, we lost our distinctiveness as a church. We put time and effort into making the church accessible to the nonchurched. But this greater accessibility came at a price. We weren't really an alternative community with countercultural values. We were a composite of suburban America, consumerism and Jesus. We blended right in.

We've pondered how we can gain a hearing for the gospel of the kingdom in a comfortable suburban culture where there are few real needs. Perhaps a national disaster would topple the scaffolding on which many stand secure and give them ears to hear. If our recent economic crisis deepened and we found ourselves in the second great depression, perhaps people would hunger for good news. Perhaps the radically changed lives of Christ followers would gain a hearing with the nonchurched. But how radical would it have to be for anyone to notice? Would individual character makeovers arouse the interest of the perpetually distracted? If we truly lived the way we believe, people would surely pay more attention. If Christians were actually different from the world, the world might want to know why. Or maybe, if the church actually were an alternative community driven by countercultural, kingdom values, maybe the world would investigate. Perhaps a miracle is the answer. Massive numbers of people being healed from diseases and raised from the dead would likely pry open eyes and ears.

There is a couple in our church that is trying to push this issue of an alternative community to new and delightfully disturbing levels. They are exploring the idea of sharing resources with a few other families. Each family willingly surrenders a convenience like the cars, washer, Internet or refrigerator, and depends on the other families to supply the help. Perhaps this is the kind of radical community that will arouse the interest of our seeking friends. We believe groups of people actually living differently together can be a powerful witness for the gospel.

We aren't sure what it exactly looks like. But to be effective in reaching the world, we probably have to entertain more radical ideas of what it means to be the church and to live in community.

Releasing results. Inviting without obsessing over the results has become another important aspect of our evangelism. We aren't responsible for the outcome of our evangelistic work. It's not our job to cram the gospel down the throat of the uninterested in the hope of coercing a decision out of them. It's not our job to close the sale. Hospitality to the nonchurched means we invite them to explore and consider life under Jesus. We do this in a variety of ways. There are some who are ready to follow Christ, and we should boldly and graciously invite them to make that decision. Others we invite to dinner at our house. We get together for coffee and ask questions. We create a space where they can tell their story. We listen to them. Perhaps we invite them to join us in a service project in the community. Maybe we invite them to an event or retreat at the church. The point is to align with what God is already doing in them rather than making it our agenda to "save them."

THE ROLE OF THE CHURCH

Imagine having a series of spiritual conversations at a local pub with a handful of Christians and their seeking friends. Suppose God is genuinely at work in the hearts of both groups. They are both awakening from a long sleep. They are both in the process of converting. They are seekers discovering God. The Christians are rediscovering the radical difference Jesus can make in daily life. There is ongoing Bible study, prayer and relationship. The conversation is rich. The group serves together at the local soup kitchen. Each seeker is responding, and they keep asking, "What's next?" It makes sense that somewhere in the process there is an invitation to participate in the life of a church. This group, as good as it is, is not the church.

At some point, we must invite our friends into a community of faith where there is teaching, worship, prayer, the Lord's Supper, submission and diverse relationships. They need to gather with others who are different—who don't necessarily agree with them and don't see the world the way they do—to worship God. They need to hear God's Word. They need to participate in the sharing of God's story. They need to receive the sacraments. They need to experience dissatisfaction and disappointment with their leaders and learn how to respond maturely and with grace. In evangelism we are not only inviting people to follow Jesus. We are inviting people to do so in community with others. We are inviting them into a faith community where the gospel is being imperfectly lived out.

I have a friend I've known since we were fifteen. He is one of my best friends. He lives in another state, so we only see each other once or twice a year. When we get together, we golf and I trounce him in video games. I became a Christ follower when I was nineteen while living in a dorm room with him in college. Over the years we've had numerous spiritual conversations. I'm not sure where he is in his relationship with Jesus. Regardless, I will be his friend for life.

A few years ago I officiated at his wedding. I had wonderful conversations with him and his fiancée in premarital counseling. In the midst of these discussions, I often encouraged them to start attending church services on a regular basis. It just made sense that if they were going pursue God with any degree of intentionality, they needed to pick a church and start participating in it. I asked them to commit to attend a church of their choice for at least three months after they were married. I can't imagine anything better for their ongoing search for God.

Of course it will be an imperfect experience. People in the church will act weird. They will do things and say things the couple won't understand. The sermons might fly over their heads. The singing will be uncomfortable. But I can't imagine anything better for their spiritual life.

THE CHURCH IN A COMMUNITY

In addition to the role of an individual church in the process of evangelizing individuals, there is the role of the broader church, the overall Christian witness, in a given community. The stylistic differences, nuances and petty disagreements that separate our churches hinder our witness to the world. The undercurrent of competition between churches mimics the ideals of the world. In this system a few churches "win" while most gradually lose. Our evangelistic witness as a Christian people becomes more credible when we unite with other Christians regardless of their particular church association. This is not an easy task. Perhaps it will mean neighborhood small groups composed of Christians who live in the area rather than Christians only from our church. Perhaps it means the churches of an area pool their resources in shared projects designed to bring the gospel to a community. Whatever it might practically look like, the walls of our churches will have to come down in order to reach our community with the gospel.

Our commitment to keeping the conversation going on this subject is perhaps one of the best things we've done over the past few years. It is not easy to sort out how to reach people with the gospel. There are many factors that only a few years ago were not relevant to the discussion. We have a small group of people who regularly meet to talk about the evangelism question in light of our understanding of the gospel. This helps keep the subject in front of us. It also helps sharpen our thinking as we continue to discover how to share our faith with a world that is lost.

A year or so ago a friend who is passionate about giving himself away in service to the hurting made a connection with a seeker. As he built a relationship with this seeker, it didn't take long before he realized something was stirring in this man. He continued to call him and periodically met with him. My friend then took the risk of inviting this guy to his small group. After he attended, my friend then asked him to come to a men's breakfast. The Spirit of God was clearly working in the seeker, and he continued to be drawn to God. Eventually my friend invited him to a church service. There hasn't been a moment of decision. He is not a fully participating member of our church. He has not been baptized. The man is still seeking, still sorting things out. But he is doing so in the context of an unconditional relationship with a follower of Christ. We have discovered very few answers about evangelism since making the move toward spiritual formation. But this guy represents what we want to be about. And perhaps, in the long run, it is best to not try to answer all the questions, but faithfully share the gospel in deed and word, and let God sort out the rest.

11

WORSHIP

Celebrating the Story of God

KENT CARLSON

6

I was awakened from a fitful and uneasy sleep by the sound of a clanging bell. It was 5:15 a.m. It took me a few moments to remember where I was. A friend and I had driven to a monastery on the Pacific coast for a five-day retreat of silence and solitude. The bell was calling me to the morning vigils. Retreats such as these, especially during times of frenetic activity and demanding, relentless deadlines, are not always pleasant experiences for me. At least not at first. At these retreats I am sometimes forced to face the fact that it has been too long since I have been quiet enough to have my disordered heart exposed for the mess that it is. My first day had been such an exposing. I struggled with loneliness, sadness, insecurity, and a deep sense of disconnection from God and others. I wanted to go home and immerse myself once more in the various ways I have learned to hide and numb the pain. I went to sleep instead.

At the sound of the bell I dragged myself out of bed, threw some clothes on and walked into the pitch-black darkness. It was a perfectly clear, crisp and cold November predawn morning, and the sky was filled with more stars than I had ever seen. The monastery sits at the edge of a cliff and looks out across a breathtaking expanse of ocean. Even in the darkness I could see the seemingly infinite Pacific stretching out before me.

I walked alone to the little chapel where vigils would be observed. I opened the door, and on the wall of the narthex was a famous icon of the holy Trinity. I stood there and looked at it for a minute or two. A number of others filed in during this time, and we smiled at each other as we quietly took our seats. There were just a dozen or so of us in this little chapel. Each one of us had unplugged for a few days from the craziness of daily life, hoping for a dose of eternal reality. We all sat in the candle-lit silence with a deep sense of anticipation.

One by one, quietly, the white-robed, bareheaded monks began to enter. For some unknown reason I found it fascinating that they were all wearing blue jeans and tennis shoes. Perhaps I thought that the clothing under their robes should be a bit more religious. Upon further reflection I found myself appreciating this. They seemed more real to me this way.

After a moment or two they began to chant the Psalms, and without any effort I found I was giving myself fully to the moment. I believed everything they were chanting with a deeper way of believing than I was used to. One of the monks looked at me and smiled, and to my great surprise he walked over and sat next to me and showed me how to follow along, inviting me to worship with him and his brother monks and this small gathering of Christ followers. The opening hymn went like this:

O ever-blessed Trinity
You order everything you made.
Our days for work, our nights for rest,
A peaceful round to be obeyed.

Happy we come to give you praise
Before we start to live our day

Joining our hearts to every song
All living creatures sing and pray.

Three in one and one in Three
O teach us how to live that we,
With all who sleep and wake to love,
May come to perfect liberty.

In this little chapel on the West Coast I chanted psalms with these unknown monks and fellow worshipers, and together we declared these universe-altering truths about this God-invaded planet. All of us believed these words, trusted them and sought to root our lives in them. I was overwhelmed by the sacred gift of this moment.

As I joined my voice with these singing monks, we were bearing witness to the truth that there is a grand and glorious story infinitely bigger than the small story of our individual lives. In community with a small band of Christ followers I didn't even know, I found myself being slowly liberated—rescued, saved—by this story. My lonely, solitary life has a deep and abiding meaning and significance as it is immersed in this astonishing story of God's redemption. This amazed me; I was lifted outside of my smallness and was rooted in something huge and immensely powerful.

Worship, at its most basic, is a celebration and a retelling of the story of God. Our lives are bombarded with messages from a noisy world that declares with relentless constancy that our lives are about us, our wants, our desires, our needs. Worship, at its best, exposes this oppressive self-absorption and invites us to root the smaller story of our lives into the larger story of God's ongoing redemption of humanity and this universe. My early morning celebration of vigils recalibrated the focus of my life and reminded me that my life will find its truest meaning and significance not in narcissistic self-absorption but in remembering and rehearsing the story of God.

CONSUMERISM AND WORSHIP

From the very beginning of our journey to restructure our church around helping people to reorient their lives around the teachings of Jesus, we knew that public worship would be a foundational area we had to address. Perhaps nowhere else in the church does our consumeristic bent rear its ugly head more obviously than here. Most churchgoers have pretty strong opinions about what they like and dislike in worship, and they make their opinions known by their attendance. Most church leaders know what 60 to 70 percent of the churchgoers in their particular "target group" prefer in worship. All we have to do is provide that "worship style" with excellence and we will be relatively successful at getting our share of that market. We can be an alternative jazz radio station if we want, but we will never reach as many people as a station that plays the top forty. There is a worship style that has become predominant in suburban evangelical America, and if we deviate too greatly from it, we will lose our share of the market.

At Oak Hills we sensed that we would never do a very good job of inviting people to reorient their lives around the teachings of Christ if our worship services became simply another place where Christians exercised their consumer choices. Inevitably this would lead to worship centered around personal tastes and the primacy of the worshipers' experience rather than the story of God. So we intentionally marched into this area with the grace and discernment of a bull in a china shop. We made many mistakes, admittedly, but we were committed to orienting our worship services around the story of God, not the stylistic preferences of the worshiper. We're still trying to figure this out.

THE STYLE DILEMMA

Before I get too far into this, let me offer a disclaimer. There is an inherent judgmentalism in any critique of public worship in our culture. High-brow worshipers, with their more classical preferences, are not somehow more mature in their worship than those who have never met a contemporary worship chorus they do not love. A string quartet in a Gothic cathedral is not somehow more "worshipful" (to use an odd and almost completely useless word) than a guitar-driven garage band in some rented retail space.

Mature worshipers know that worship is about the story of God, not our particular preferences. Therefore, when I gather with other followers of Christ to worship God, I best leave my judgments and my preferences at home, and humbly submit myself to the style of worship before me. There is something arrogant and contrary to the Spirit of Christ to coldly and dispassionately judge either the quality or the appropriateness of a worship service we are attending. There is no problem with having stylistic preferences and to even believe that one style is somewhat better than another. There is, though, a great problem with placing style at the center of worship and being unable to worship in a style different from my own.

God is inclined to look at the heart of the worshiper, his or her engagement in the worship and willingness to be immersed in the story of God. Certainly some church worship services are less conducive to centering us around the story of God. But this is less often a stylistic issue and more commonly an indication of that church's lack of a well-developed theology of worship.

Judgmentalism in this area came home to me at a worship service at our church several years ago. I could not control my irritation at how the worship service was going and at the stylistic preferences of the person who was leading worship that day. I was confident that my irritation was related to what I foolishly thought was my higher and more mature understanding of worship. In hindsight, however, I realize that my irritation was centered primarily on style.

As our congregation was standing and singing, I stood there with my hands in my pockets and my head down. I had thoughts of rushing the stage and tackling the guy who was leading us. Just then I glanced over at a couple who have been a part of our church for over two decades. I knew them well. They had been through all sorts of tragedies and had endured all sorts of changes and challenges at the church. And there they stood, arms around each other's waists, and their other hands held high in the air, singing their hearts out, absolutely in love with God. The thought that someone near them was too mature to lose himself in this moment would have been a total absurdity to them. An immediate sense of shame flooded over me.

I was the immature worshiper, not the guy up front. I was stuck in my own story, obsessed with my own preferences, oblivious to the story of God. I forced myself to take my hands out of my pockets and stick them up in the air and fully engage in the worship of God. That experience has changed my perspective on worship styles. No matter what is happening in a worship service, my job as a worshiper is not to critique but rather to give myself fully to God and to immerse the smaller story of my life into the larger story of God's redemption.

Disclaimer aside, what we do in our public worship does matter. Our worship services clearly declare what we believe about God and our relationship with him. In addition, as Marva Dawn writes, "Every aspect of the time we spend together in the worshiping Christian community influences the kind of people we are becoming." In other words, our worship services will form us into a certain kind of person. If our worship services are centered on the story of God, we will be assisted in becoming men and women whose lives are more deeply rooted in God. If our worship services are centered around our personal tastes, needs and desires, they will become merely another place that props up our inherent self-absorption.

In his marvelous book *Worship Old and New*, Robert Webber has a chapter titled "Content, Structure and Style." This helps us understand what goes into our worship services. Webber argues that the order of content, structure and style is of supreme importance. The content of our worship must come first. Then we must intentionally draw on a structure that is best suited to deliver the content. Finally, style, or the atmosphere of our worship, is the last thing to be considered. I agree with him. Regretfully, in most evangelical churches the order is reversed and style leads the way. The atmosphere of the room, the choice of music, the personality of the worship leader, the level of formality or informality, the degree of expressed emotion are style matters seen as foundational. We sought to address this at Oak Hills. We're still working on it.

PRIORITIZING THE CONTENT OF WORSHIP

Let's consider content first. This is rather simple and straightforward. Our worship services are centered on telling and celebrating the biblical story of God creating and redeeming this world. The story is delivered as a three-way dialogue: God speaks to us, we speak to God, and we speak to each other. There are declarations and responses. Our worship services declare how God has initiated and continues to bring about the salvation of fallen humanity. And we respond in adoration and praise. Therefore, in worship we remember the story of Abraham and the creation of the Hebrew nation. We remember Israel's deliverance from Egypt, the giving of the law, the inheritance of the Promised Land, the establishment of the monarchy, the exile of Israel and Judah, and the call of the prophets to return to God. We recount the story of the birth, life, teachings, death, resurrection and ascension of Jesus. We tell the story of the church and celebrate the sure and certain return of Christ to make all things new. We celebrate God's continual activity in this world and his invitation to join with him in his plan of redemption. This wonderful story, with the extensive scriptural teaching on the implications of all this, is the central content of our worship.

The primacy of this content in worship may seem like an obvious truth and one that would be enthusiastically embraced by all churches. In actual practice, though, much of the worship content in evangelical churches centers around our needs and our desires. In our seeker-service days, even in our midweek New Community, we emphasized creating meaningful experiences and pragmatic instruction for daily life. After our Donner Party experience we attempted to address this by focusing our worship services around the story of God.

One woman who had become a follower of Christ through our seeker services in the mid-1990s, quit coming to our worship services after the change. I ran into her at a social gathering and asked her where she had been. She told me, in her wonderfully candid manner, that the worship services now seemed boring and did not fill her with the same good feelings she used to have. She wasn't that interested in all the details of the story of Israel and all that other "Bible stuff." She asked me when we were going to do another series on marriage, parenting, relationships or any number of the other "felt need" emphases that were our standard fare during the 1990s.

I explained that we were addressing all those important issues, but we believed it was crucial to center our worship around the story of God. We wanted to emphasize what God has done and is doing to redeem our world.

She smiled and said, "I suppose that's good, but I guess it just isn't that interesting to me."

Her refreshingly direct comment had a profound effect on me. I found myself wondering what this woman had actually committed herself to when she had become a follower of Christ. Had she simply enjoyed the good experiences and the practical teaching she received at our church, but had little interest in God? It was painfully obvious that this woman believed that the worship services were to be designed for her.

Another more subtle aspect of content makes this issue all the more complicated. It is unfair and inaccurate to characterize all contemporary evangelical worship as being oriented around the needs of the worshiper. In truth, the best examples of contemporary evangelical worship emphasize wholehearted and intensely sincere expressions of praise to God.

Joe Horness, a contributing author in the book *Exploring the Worship Spectrum*, argues that what God desires in worship is that we are fully engaged. "What I think God cares about," Horness writes, "is the disengaged heart. . . . Worship that is not heartfelt and authentic simply does not interest him." Horness builds his case by quoting from Isaiah:

> These people come near me with their mouth
>   and honor me with their lips,
>   but their hearts are far from me.
> Their worship of me
>   is based on merely human rules they have been taught.
> (Isaiah 29:13)

Certainly Horness makes a crucially important point here. No one would argue that worship can be divorced from our wholehearted engagement in the act of praise. Listless, disengaged and mindless worship seems entirely inconsistent with a worshiper who authentically hungers for God. I believe, though, that there are two issues that need to be addressed.

First, the context of this passage in Isaiah emphasizes not the sincerity of the worshiper but more foundationally the lives we live outside our worship services. God hates even our most sincere worship when we neglect issues of justice and the needs of our neighbor. Isaiah says,

> When you come to appear before me,
>   who has asked this of you,
>   this trampling of my courts?
> Stop bringing meaningless offerings!
>   Your incense is detestable to me.
> New Moons, Sabbaths and convocations—
>   I cannot bear your evil assemblies.
> Your New Moon feasts and your appointed festivals
>   I hate with all my being.
> They have become a burden to me;
>   I am weary of bearing them.
> When you spread out your hands in prayer,
>   I will hide my eyes from you;
> even if you offer many prayers,
>   I will not listen.
> Your hands are full of blood;
>   wash and make yourself clean.
> Take your evil deeds
>   out of my sight!
> Stop doing wrong,
>   learn to do right!
> Seek justice,

encourage the oppressed.
Defend the cause of the fatherless,
   plead the case of the widow. (Isaiah 1:12-17)

This prophetic word is not centered on how engaged we are in the worship service. In truth, God is saying almost the opposite. He is saying, quite clearly, "I see your raised hands and hear your many prayers, but these mean nothing to me. I hate them, as long as you ignore justice and the needs of the oppressed." As Mark Labberton writes in his extraordinary book *The Dangerous Act of Worship*,

> For all of our apparent passion about God, in the end much of our worship seems to be mostly about us. We presume we can worship in a way that will find God but lose track of our neighbor. Yet it was this very pattern in Israel's worship life that brought God's judgment. Biblical worship that finds God will also find our neighbor.

There is, though, a second and more subtle difficulty with this emphasis by Horness. When we place our sincerity and wholeheartedness at the center of our worship, the content of our worship will drift toward how well we are doing with our wholehearted worship. The danger is that worship will gradually become a performance. Rather than being centered on the story of God, worship is centered on the intensity of our sincerity and devotion.

Webber argues that no one can consistently perform at that level of intensity and authenticity in worship. Worship must be centered on what God has done and is doing for us, not what we are doing for him. Webber writes,

> This is the message that is missing in the literature of contemporary worship. It is too much about what I ought to do and too little about what God has done for me. God has done for me what I cannot do for myself. He did it in Jesus Christ. Therefore my worship is offered in a broken vessel that is in the process of being healed, but is not yet capable of fullness of joy, endless

intense passion, absolute exaltation, and celebration. But Jesus, who shares my humanity yet without sin, is not only my Savior—he is also my complete and eternal worship, doing for me, in my place, what I cannot do.

Again, let me be clear in emphasizing that I am not arguing that authentic expressions of worship should be cold, distant or detached. When we gather to worship, we should engage our entire selves fully in the experience. But our engagement cannot be the central thing about worship. The central thing—the content of our worship—is the story of God, not our sincerity.

It is demonstrably obvious that one of the main problems of contemporary evangelical worship is that we are weak on the content side. Our informal liturgy is usually highly extemporaneous and heavily tilted toward our personal expressions of love and praise. The typical contemporary worship chorus is not often a deep source of biblical truth. We do not usually draw on centuries of rich biblical and liturgical content to inform our worship. This often leads to what I refer to as the *tyranny of the sincere*. Since our worship services aren't centered on content that is true regardless of our engagement, we make up for this by demonstrating that we "really, really" mean what we are singing. This can be a heavy burden, not only for the worshiper but also for the worship leader. Nobody can worship with that intensity every week. The danger of feigned sincerity becomes very high. It is a great comfort to me to know that when I gather to worship with other followers of Christ, the primary issue is not how well I am worshiping but that what God has done and is doing for us in Christ is central. To the best of my ability, I am seeking to root my individual life in that story.

Scripture demands that we place the activity of God, not our experience, sincerity or devotion, at the center of worship. We intentionally addressed this issue at Oak Hills. We began to read more Scripture in our services. We experimented with responsive readings of psalms. We incorporated ancient, content-rich prayers. We recited the creeds. We began to use the church calendar to help us enter more fully into the story of God. Because of these added elements in our worship services, we had to shorten some of the other aspects of our service. We seldom had the time to string together four or five choruses in a row (what is known in some circles as a "worship set"). For many, this extended singing time was the most meaningful part of the worship service, and taking time to more fully declare and celebrate the story of God simply did not matter to them. They felt a sense of loss.

This raises an important question. Is our worship centered on God and his story, or on my devotion and authentic praise? Obviously, we hope both aspects are present in our worship, but in a culture that is clearly oriented around the insatiable demands of the self, we must make certain that our worship begins with and is built around the story of God. Worship is primarily about what God has done and is doing through Christ.

THE STRUCTURE OF THE WORSHIP SERVICE

Once the content of worship has been addressed, we are free to move on to the issue of structure. This deals with how we organize the worship service, the ingredients included and what order we put them in. At Oak Hills we decided to follow Webber's suggestion to use the four common movements of worship in the history of the church: the gathering, the service of the Word, the service of the Table and the sending.

Gathering. The gathering involves the recognition that we come to worship from all walks of life and with a variety of life experiences. We recognize that while we come to worship as individuals, we are called to worship as a local expression of the unified body of Christ. This process of coming to worship, or gathering, needs to be respected and given sufficient time. A call to worship and a time of invoking God's blessing is included. During this time we usually sing with joy in our hearts as we call each other to worship God.

Service of the Word. The service of the Word is oriented around

Scripture, which is the ultimate authority for followers of Christ. It includes such ingredients as Scripture readings, interviews with people, various multimedia presentations, dramatic sketches and other creative elements, and, of course, the sermon. During this time we also seek to provide opportunity for people to respond, in some creative manner, to our encounter with God's Word.

Service of the Table. The service of the Table is our monthly celebration of the Lord's Supper, when we tell the story of God's redemptive work through Christ, give thanks to God and partake of the elements together. We celebrate and draw spiritual sustenance from the very real presence of Christ in this meal.

Sending. The sending is a reminder that we are ambassadors of Christ and are sent into the world to declare the good news of God's redemption. In the sending portion of our service we are reminded that worship has a missional aspect, for there is no real worship without a corresponding intention to "do justice and to love mercy." In the sending we ask God's blessing on us as we go out and serve the world, which is precious to him.

In addition to these four movements we also include a number of other elements that change from time to time. We often include "Acts of Praise," during which we engage our voices, our bodies and our emotions in expressions of our love and devotion to God. This time includes singing choruses and hymns, responsive readings, the offering and other ways to declare God's greatness and express our thanks.

In addition, we will often include a time called "Community," in which we make announcements, have extended greeting times, baptize, dedicate children to the Lord and take other opportunities to celebrate the truth that we're a family.

Throughout this structure we use many creative and artistic expressions, by both the worship leadership and the worshipers themselves. We believe the arts create marvelous opportunities to call the community of Christ followers together to worship God with our whole being. Music, dance, video, painting, drama and poetry are used throughout this structure to help us celebrate the story of God.

The worship of the gathered community of Christ followers is a wonderful place for artists to serve the body of Christ.

This structure provides us with a skeleton on which we can build the body of our worship service. Far from putting us into some kind of straightjacket, this structure provides a solid and coherent rationale for what we do during worship. There is a constant dialogue between God and his people. He speaks to us and we respond to him. While I believe the structure we use is historically consistent with the practice of the church, it's not the only legitimate structure. The key is to have an intentional structure on which to build the content of our worship.

THE STYLE OF WORSHIP

Finally, there's the issue of style. A fascinating thing happened to those of us who plan worship at Oak Hills. We discovered that when we nailed down the issues of content and structure, style became less divisive. We discovered that our discomfort with a particular style of worship was intensified when we were not confident that our content and our structure had integrity. But when we knew we were developing content-rich and structurally sound worship services, we felt free to use the style most natural to us.

For twenty-five years the worship style at Oak Hills has been patterned after the typical evangelical contemporary worship service: primarily informal, band-driven, emotive and with a heavy emphasis on worship choruses. This is our bread and butter. If we deviate too greatly from this comfortable and natural style, people get nervous. The beauty of paying attention to the issues of content, structure and style is that when style is less important, we can stop arguing over it.

My own worship-style preference would not be centered around a band with backup singers and a heavy worship-chorus emphasis. Though I don't mind that style of worship, and there are many times when I find myself thoroughly enjoying it, I am more comfortable in a quieter, subdued and liturgically rich worship style. But here is the wonderful and liberating truth: that's just my style, and style should be the last consideration.

We still have much to learn at Oak Hills about public worship. We have made many mistakes and will undoubtedly make many more. This past decade has been one long season of experimenting and trying to figure it out. Our church has been wonderfully patient with us along the way. Still, we have found great liberation in focusing our worship services around the story of God and his redemption. After much upheaval, our congregation, to a large extent, has embraced this shift, and for this I am deeply grateful.

12

MISTAKES

After Further Review

MIKE LUEKEN

❧

*I*n the midst of a particularly exhausting season during the past decade, complaints began flooding in over what was happening at the weekend services. At the time we still had our midweek New Community service on Thursday nights. I remember getting wind of these complaints one Thursday afternoon. The theme was "These services aren't doing anything for me anymore." I remember the surge of anger that coursed through me. I should have taken a walk or a nap or a long bubble bath. Instead, I made the moronic decision to publicly respond at that evening's service. I was tired of the complaints.

That afternoon, I angrily scratched out a new sermon on a yellow pad. For thirty-five minutes I railed against consumerism. It was a woodshed message. My "passion" was a poor disguise for my anger. What I said was true and perhaps needed to be said. Some good came out of the message. But I was preaching in anger. It was a foolish decision.

It took us nearly ten years to restructure our church around spiritual formation. It's been a fascinating journey. And at the risk of sounding arrogant, we are proud of the road we have traveled. We are humbled by God's steadfast faithfulness. We are in awe of the congregation's gracious trust in following our lead on an uncharted course. Many times during this last decade we led with gentle strength and made wise decisions. But we made plenty of mistakes as well. There is no way to minimize or excuse those mistakes. In some cases these were costly. They hurt real people and shook their confidence in the institution of the church. Relationships were fractured. Undoubtedly, some may even have had their faith shaken by our stupidity.

LEADING UNLIKE CHRIST

Christian leaders usually put too much weight on external outcomes. We often fall into the trap of evaluating spiritual work by numbers. We graph the attendance. We count the offerings. We compare current statistics to the previous years. External results are an unreliable guide. In spite of what some statistics may show, the church in America faces an uncertain future. The landscape is rapidly changing. New questions are being asked. Old "givens" are being challenged. One of those "givens," our paradigm of success, needs an overhaul. Our instincts need to be retrained. We need to learn to think counterintuitively. Declining attendance may actually be a sign of God's blessing. Decreased offerings may be the result of an exceptional leadership decision. The loss of momentum may be God's way of exposing our hidden attachments and deepening our dependency on him. Outward success may cost too high of a price. Decisions that negatively impact the bottom line are not necessarily mistakes.

Obviously, it's pretty easy to be an armchair quarterback. The privileged vantage point of our favorite recliner and the technology of TiVo affords us the ability to rewind every play and critique every player as if we actually know something about professional football. While we've been doing single arm curls with a pizza slice, these world-class athletes have trained rigorously to play their sport at the highest level. Still, we scream at them for throwing an errant pass. I guess it's our right as fans. But some of us actually live in the illusion that we could do better. It's always easy to second-guess when we have the luxury of time to reflect on the alternatives. But it's a different story when we are in the heat of the battle and have two seconds to make a decision.

When I think about our mistakes over these past ten years, I think of those times when we responded poorly to a person who did not align with our agenda. These kinds of leadership mistakes are particularly worth noting and attending to because they are rooted in our character. They emerge from who we are. What do we do when we don't get what we want? How do we respond to people whose words or actions chip away at our identity?

In general terms this is the most obvious and repeated mistake we made. Simply stated, at times we were unlike Christ. We were proud. We overreacted. We lacked grace. Perhaps it's a cheap confession to say we didn't always lead like Jesus. It's a superb example of stating the obvious. But it points to the ironic fact that while we were trying to lead our church toward spiritual formation, we encountered numerous situations that exposed our unformedness. The complaints, resistance and opposition revealed the cracks in our hearts. We knew from the outset that the first priority after the Donner retreat was to be purposeful in our own spiritual formation. But transformation takes time. It's impossible to hurry up and become more like Jesus. For much of this transition we were leading beyond ourselves.

A LITANY OF ERRORS

Soon after the Donner experience we went to work to change the DNA of Oak Hills. There were hundreds of people who had sacrificed time, money and energy to grow the church and reach our community with the gospel. They had supported the seeker strategy. They loved what was happening at Oak Hills. They were excited about the completion of our first permanent building and looking forward to the next season in our adventure. Then we made a hard right turn. Our shift in focus caught them off-guard. Things began to change, quite literally, overnight. The suddenness made people wonder whether their investment of time and money in the seeker strategy was a waste of time.

We fueled these doubts. These were long-time evangelical Christians. In addition to changing direction, part of our deconstruction was a blitzkrieg on evangelicalism. We questioned its subculture. For some we were challenging lifelong beliefs about the gospel, the church, worship and discipleship. We didn't grasp how unsettling this was for people. We were slaughtering their sacred cows right in front of their eyes. In reality, our message was mostly on target. We absolutely needed to make changes, and there was no good way to ease into them. But we didn't always do a good job of walking in their shoes. We lacked compassion. We were impatient. We were inattentive to those who were confused. Perhaps, at some level, we drove the change too much from the top down without doing the hard work of bringing people along with us.

Most people were not obstinate. They were willing to follow our lead, but they needed time to sort through the issues. They needed time to work through their questions. They needed our help, and many times we patiently tried. But too often we viewed them as opponents instead of taking the time to listen. Perhaps we were threatened by their hesitation to get onboard. I know it wasn't long before I suffered from "transition fatigue."

Impatient leadership. There was no way to sidestep some of the tough decisions that needed to be made. We weren't going to make this shift without some pain. But we could have done a better job of patiently leading our people away from the old and into the new.

In thinking about leadership mistakes in the context of our transition, the issue is far more complicated than a mythical right-and-wrong paradigm, or what we should or should not have done. We should have been more like Jesus. But that sounds like a Sunday school answer. We were impatient precisely because we were impatient. We led in a way that was perfectly consistent with who we were, in our hearts, at that point. Again, this is not to minimize what we did or didn't do. It is to remind us of the "narrow road" we must travel if we intend to be better leaders.

Wordiness. A transition of this magnitude required hours of conversations and interaction to flesh out the implications of the changes we were making. But our impatience with people showed in our wordiness. We talked too much. We were frivolous with words and stingy with silence. Perhaps a hazard of Christian leadership is we don't learn how to listen. We spend inordinate amounts of time trying to inspire people to do what they may not want to do. We're always trying to persuade. We're constantly answering questions. We are doling out counsel. We pontificate. People would have benefited from having more of our ears and less of our mouths. There's "a time to be silent and a time to speak" (Ecclesiastes 3:7).

I remember one occasion when someone was furious with one of our decisions. The person could not contain her emotion. I should have let her unload. Compassionate silence may have created space for her to work through it. But I went on the offensive. I argued our point. I pushed back on her "flawed" reasoning. I said some things I still regret.

Praying too little. Henri Nouwen writes:

> For the future of Christian leadership it is of vital importance to reclaim the mystical aspect of theology so that every word spoken, every word of advice given, every strategy developed can come from a heart that knows God intimately. . . .
>
> Christian leaders cannot simply be persons who have well-informed opinions about the burning issues of our time. Their leadership must be rooted in the permanent, intimate relationship with the incarnate Word, Jesus, and they need to find there the source for their words, advice, and guidance. Through the discipline of contemplative prayer, Christian leaders have to learn to listen again and again to the voice of love and to find there the wisdom and courage to address whatever issue presents itself to them. Dealing with burning issues without being

rooted in a deep personal relationship with God easily leads to divisiveness because, before we know it, our sense of self is caught up in our opinion about a given subject. But when we are securely rooted in personal intimacy with the source of life, it will be possible to remain flexible without being relativistic, convinced without being rigid, willing to confront without being offensive, gentle and forgiving without being soft, and true witnesses without being manipulative.

These remarks by Nouwen are profoundly challenging. At Oak Hills we have a proclivity for careful thinking, offering our opinions about "the burning issues of our time" and talking. This is good. Obviously these are necessary skills for effective pastoral leadership. Christian leadership requires diligent work to sort through the complex maze of new ideas, challenges and opportunities. There are many more books to read than time to read them. The church is a living organism constantly adapting to the rapidly changing cultural milieu. It is virtually impossible to keep up with the onslaught of information.

We spent countless hours reading whatever we could find and conversing about the various issues surrounding our transition to spiritual formation. Our understanding was clarified through the process. But not only did we talk too soon and too much, we prayed too little. This is why Nouwen's words are so important. We often made the mistake of "dealing with the burning issues" of our transition "without being rooted in a deep personal relationship with God." This sounds so churchy. It sounds like the obligatory prayer card. I'm not even sure I fully understand what this would have looked like. But the raging chaos of this transition was a prime occasion to "remain in the vine" (John 15:4). I know there where times when I felt like I had allowed myself to be severed from the vine. I was relying on my own wisdom. My sense of self was caught up in my opinion about a subject. I was inflexible. My confidence and conviction was in my intuitive and often arrogant belief that I was right.

This "mistake" is not restricted to the isolated situation of our transition. It is a persistent weakness of our ministry. But the stakes were high when we decided to change our church. I would like to have spent more energy in contemplative prayer so my public interactions were more "securely rooted in personal intimacy with the source of life."

Spiritual elitism. We had spent the decade preceding Donner diligently trying to reach nonchurched people with the gospel. God was faithful, and honored our attentiveness to those outside his family. The church was externally focused. This was one of the many benefits of being seeker-driven.

For the first few years after Donner we were laser focused on the individual's journey toward Christlikeness. The ministries we initiated to foster growth were designed to get people thinking about their past, their life story and the specific areas of their character needing spiritual growth. We unpacked the details behind anger, lust, worry and fear. We taught on solitude, silence and spending time alone with God. We warned of the danger of hurry. We encouraged people to slow down so they could attend to God in the present moment. We had always been known as a church that valued humor and laughter. But now we were serious and somber most of the time.

All of this was good. We needed to be more purposeful about helping individuals grow. There are supposed to be identifiable differences between those who follow Jesus and those who don't. But in the process we nurtured a subculture of elitism within the church. We mistakenly forgot about the needs of the lost. Two unofficial camps formed: those who got it, and those who didn't; the enlightened and the unenlightened; the serious Christian and the "pretender." For years Oak Hills was a safe place for those who were investigating the claims of Christianity. There was ample room to come and explore at a comfortable pace. But now, those who were not ready for the rigorous road of transformation felt like they were on the outside of a "special" group. The person who enjoyed extended time in solitude and silence felt affirmed. The activists looked for a hiding place. The high-church liturgy lover was applauded. The contemporary-worship fans wore paper bags on their heads. The intentional Christ follower was "in." The seeker and marginally committed were "out." This was a costly mistake with consequences that extended for years.

When spiritual formation is a priority, sectarian elitism is a risk. It is the dark side of spiritual formation. We don't need much prompting to drift into judging others. If the conditions are right, let the games begin. We have the spiritual gift of competitive comparison. So it is always crucial to keep distinguishing between genuine spiritual formation and proficiency at the various means and methods we use to do our part in that process. Spiritual maturity is becoming more like Jesus. It is not how comfortable I am spending time alone in a room staring at a candle. The substance of who we are becoming is what matters.

People who are at home in the liturgy and who "excel" in the disciplines can be spiritual snobs. Sometimes those who think they are maturing in their relationship with Jesus feel justified in distancing themselves from the broader community of the church. We saw this happen at Oak Hills. They attend the services less frequently. They don't serve in the mundane. They stand back and stroke their chin. They call it contemplation, but it's really evaluation. They reek with an arrogance that is incompatible with their alleged spiritual maturity. Recent research has shown that the "spiritually mature" are more likely to leave their church because they are not being "fed" or sufficiently challenged. Huh? How can the "spiritually mature" still be so driven by their own fickle preferences that they would leave their church because their needs aren't being met? This sounds like the definition of spiritual immaturity. Somewhere in the process of dying to self they forgot to die to their need for satisfaction.

The church will always be a melting pot of diverse people with varying levels of hunger and motivation. It has to be a place where seekers find the freedom and grace to pursue the truth of the Christian faith. In fact, one indicator that we are effectively training disciples to Jesus is that they are growing in their love for seekers and their passion to bring them to Christ. The spiritually mature love the lost. They sacrificially serve those who are not yet ready for transformation. They are at the vanguard of service to the poor and forgotten. They give ridiculous amounts of their money to God's work in this world. They stack the chairs, wipe down tables and wipe babies' butts. They complain the least. They take a vow of stability and refuse to leave the church regardless of what happens.

Deconstruction. We also made the mistake of spending too much time and energy talking about what we "weren't going to be" without describing what we were going to be. We got stuck in deconstruction. We declared war on the monster of consumerism. We elaborated on the ways it contaminates our souls. It was a battle we needed to fight. But we fought it too long without offering alternatives. Perhaps this deconstruction was necessary in order to break deep-rooted addictions. But while the deconstruction helped establish a new DNA at Oak Hills, it wore people out. People wanted to know where we were heading. For a long time, we only knew what we didn't want to be.

The deconstruction brought change through subtraction rather than addition. We eliminated services and ministries people appreciated before we were ready to introduce new ones oriented around spiritual formation. Even if we didn't know exactly what the future was going to look like, we would have served the church better by offering some practical ways of implementing our new emphasis or at least delaying drastic changes to programs and ministries until alternatives were ready to be introduced.

Publicizing our angst. Oak Hills has always been a church fiercely committed to risky authenticity. Our congregation routinely hears about the imperfections of their pastors. There is a lot of material to work with. We've also had a few morality issues through the years that we chose to share with the congregation as honestly as possible. People who have been part of Oak Hills for a while would likely identify authenticity as one of the church's strengths.

But there can be a downside to authenticity in a high-stakes transition like the one at Oak Hills. As we waded through the changes, our heads were spinning. We were not only considering new, paradigm-shifting ideas, but we were gradually worn down by the complaints and criticisms. At so many levels, layers were unraveling faster within us and the church than we could process. At times we were not doing well. We were irritated with religious consumerism. We were worried about finances. We were questioning the purpose of the church. We played a lot of this out in public settings. Many appreciated our honesty. But others were scared and confused by it. Given all that was at stake, I think it would have been wise to be more measured.

CHOOSING NOT TO WALLOW

We are practitioners. We do not sit in the ivory tower of the consultant's chair. We do not stand behind the professor's lectern. Our leadership happens on the front lines of church ministry, where bullets fly. We make many decisions, and most of them directly impact our staff and congregation to one degree or another.

Mistakes are inevitable. They can be valuable. It has been a helpful, though sometimes painful, exercise to identify the mistakes we made during our transition. It's important to own these mistakes, and putting them on paper helps us do that. The alternative is to unreflectively brush them aside. At the same time, we have not spent time wallowing in guilt. We made many mistakes, and we will make many more in the future. God is bigger than our flaws and failures. Our mistakes have helped us learn valuable lessons about leadership, ministry and our own hearts. At least we hope they have.

EPILOGUE

A Vision for the Future

KENT CARLSON

6

As I reflect on the fascinating journey we have traveled this past decade, it strikes me that in many ways Mike and I have come full circle in our understanding of the church. We have gone through seasons of extreme disillusionment that at times bordered on cynicism. We have wrestled with the value of giving ourselves so wholeheartedly to an institution that seems so fatally flawed and so enmeshed with a culture that has set itself against the ways of God. In our idealism and our arrogance, we have tried to figure out a way to dismantle and then reconstruct the church so it can be everything that it is supposed to be.

After a decade of questioning almost everything we believed and understood about the church, we find ourselves stepping back and realizing that the church, as awkwardly inefficient as it often can be, is still a stunningly beautiful and powerful thing. And we love the church. We don't love some vague abstraction of the church, we love the actual church that exists in the world, and most especially that one local church God has given us the privilege to pastor.

There seems to be a tendency these days to talk and write about the church in a very abstract, theoretical, almost wispy way. Some contemporary theorists tend to picture the church as something almost indistinguishable from a handful of Christians being in the same place at the same time with a vague intention to do good. But as soon as there is any semblance of organization or programming, these theorists label it as bad, as something less than the church, a deviation from the new thing that God is doing in the world. Church programs are increasingly portrayed as the vestigial organs of a long-extinct dinosaur.

This seems unfair and irrational. It's a classic case of building a straw man and then knocking him down. The church of Jesus Christ, if it is anything, is always going to be very concrete, earthy, messy, flawed and somewhat strange. It is anything but wispy. I don't believe we can love the church of Jesus Christ in any kind of detached, abstract or theoretical way. The only way to love the church is to love and be an intimate part of a very tangible, concrete, actual, exceedingly flawed, strange, local gathering of followers of Christ.

This local gathering is indeed the only tangible expression of the universal and timeless body of Christ. There is simply no way to love this body that is spread all over the world and has stretched down through the centuries without loving an actual expression of it. Namely, the local church.

Linus, that wonderful character from Charles Schulz's *Peanuts* cartoon, attempted to love humanity in an abstract and detached way. He once famously said, "I love mankind, it's just people I can't stand." But just as there is no way to love humankind without loving actual humans, there is no way to love the universal and timeless church without loving an actual and wonderfully flawed local expression of this church.

EMBRACING THE TENSION
I have been writing this book with my very good friend Mike Lueken

during the time of the twenty-fifth anniversary of our church. Twenty-five years is a long time to be a pastor in one church. Add to that the fact that I'm the founding pastor, and it's easy to see how my roles and responsibilities are hopelessly entangled with the tiresome vestiges of institutionalism. One of the obvious and fascinating ironies of this book is that much of our critique of the contemporary church is a stinging indictment of the very specific church we have developed and continue to shepherd. We have been and continue to be part of the problem. I don't know if there is a way to escape this.

This has been a struggle for us. I find myself continually torn between my dual roles as an institutional guy *and* a radical prophet. The story of our church has attracted the attention of a number of people around the country, and we have had wonderful opportunities to gather with other church leaders to dream together about doing church in a different way. In our own geographical area, I am privileged to hang out with a number of fairly radical young Christian leaders who are starting new churches, and in these circles I'm sometimes seen as one of the most radical of the radicals. I'm one of those who are railing against the machine. I revel in this role.

Yet in my own church, I'm the institutional guy. I can't rail against the machine at Oak Hills because it's my job to keep it running. I have to pay attention to budgets, cash flow, mortgages, attendance, projections, strategic plans and various internal political issues. At night I'm a subversive revolutionary in a French café, wearing a beret and smoking cigarettes with some revolutionaries plotting the overthrow of the institutional church. The next morning I put on my nicely laundered button-down shirt, pull on my neatly pleated Dockers and drive my Honda Civic to the church office to try to figure out ways to build the organization. Sometimes it all seems a bit weird to me.

But Mike and I, and the other leaders here at Oak Hills, are learning how to live with the weirdness. We decided a few years ago that we weren't going to sell the farm. The institution matters. In fact, as we see it, there is no real church without the institution. The institution, the organization, the practical realities and the human foibles are all part of the earthy, mundane, often tiresome and yet stunningly beautiful bride of Christ. We love the real church of Jesus Christ in all its glorious imperfection. In truth, it's the only church that exists.

Having said all that, there is no doubt that the church in North America is in a time of great philosophical and institutional turmoil. When I started Oak Hills twenty-five years ago, the menu options were quite limited. The majority of evangelical churches in North America, apart from the obvious superficial differences, were essentially the same. But that has all changed. Today we have formational churches, missional churches, emergent churches, monastic community churches, house churches, unchurches, simple churches, deep churches, organic churches, ancient-future churches, not to mention the old standbys of traditional, charismatic, seeker-sensitive, seeker-targeted and seeker-driven churches.

It is increasingly obvious that we live in a transitional time in North American religious culture. The future is uncertain and many pastors and Christian leaders are struggling and groping and trying to find their way. I am fairly certain that the large, entrepreneurial, attractional model church is not the wave of the future. It is not sustainable as a model of authentic Christian community. But I truthfully am perplexed about what will replace it.

The story of Oak Hills Church reflects the story of this groping, this trying to figure it out. We became convinced that something was wrong, and we set out to find another way. But we have not arrived there yet. We're not actually sure we ever will. When we reflect on these things, we often think of Jesus' parable of the wineskins. Jesus said that "people do not pour new wine into old wineskins. If they do, the new wine will burst the skins; the wine will run out and the wineskins will be ruined. No, new wine must be poured into new wineskins" (Luke 5:37-38).

Sometimes we wonder if the reason for all of the turmoil of this past decade is that we have been trying to pour new wine into old wineskins. This has been troubling to us at times, but we have come to peace with it. If God is doing something new in our day, perhaps there will be burst wineskins all over the place. There may even be some honor in it. When you think about it, that might be a wonderful name for a church in these days. The Church of the Burst Wineskin. A church that falls apart trying to get it right might not be a failure at all. It just might be a part of the larger story of what God is doing in this world. If we have learned anything, it's not about an individual church's external success but the advancement of the kingdom of God.

ESTABLISHING BEACHHEADS

A metaphor has proven to be very useful to us for understanding this new way of looking at the church: the beachhead. (We are indebted to Dallas Willard for introducing us to this metaphor.)

A beachhead is a term describing an invading army moving onto the shore of the nation they are invading and establishing themselves in enemy territory. From this beachhead the military is able to bring in fresh troops and all the necessary supplies to establish new front lines in order to advance on the enemy. Once the beach has been taken, a command post and a field hospital are established there. And the beachhead becomes a secure place to stockpile supplies.

The only reason for the command post, field hospital and stockpile is to take care of and provide for those who are establishing new front lines in battle.

As we can well imagine, there will be those at the command post who think that this organizational headquarters exists for itself and that the stockpile is there for its own benefit. These organizational bureaucrats tend to lose sight of the fact that the only reason the command post exists is for the benefit of those on the front lines.

It is the nature of organizations to forget why they exist, and the church is always going to be an organization. But we have been given marching orders. This purpose, or our marching orders, is summed up most clearly in Matthew 28:18-20, the Great Commission. Jesus told us to go into all the world and make disciples, baptizing them into the community of the Father, the Son and the Holy Spirit, and teaching them to follow the commands of Christ. This is our job. This is what we're supposed to be doing. But perhaps we may have fallen into the trap of thinking that this Great Commission, this developing followers of Christ, is simply the job of starting churches.

At Oak Hills, we no longer believe that the task of developing churches was foremost in Jesus' mind. We believe that Jesus was referring to something similar to the concept of establishing beachheads for the kingdom of God. Planting churches undoubtedly will be a natural and necessary development of this perspective. Churches will be the organizational headquarters, the command post, the field hospital, the place where the resources are stored and given away. But our purpose is to provide followers of Christ with the necessary tools so that they can establish new front lines where the kingdom of God is breaking out.

With this perspective we have carefully studied Jesus' Sermon on the Mount (Matthew 5–7). When Jesus sits down to give a detailed, theologically rich and experientially profound sermon on what life in the kingdom of God is like, what he emphasizes is amazing. He centers his teaching on the lives of everyday people who are being profoundly transformed by his power. There's no talk of an organization. There's no building of empires. Jesus simply invites his followers to live together in the reality of God's kingdom.

Therefore, we believe that Jesus is calling us, as his disciples, as his apprentices in the art of living righteously, to establish beachheads for his kingdom, wherever God has planted us. And so the reality of the kingdom of God breaks out not so much when we gather together in the church on the weekends, although that certainly happens, but when a mother cares for her children, a carpenter frames a house, a businesswoman leads a strategic planning meeting, a mechanic tunes an engine, a student sits in class, a couple develops a relationship with their nonchurched neighbors.

We are enthralled with this vision of the kingdom of God; it's alive and active in millions of followers of Christ all over the world. The followers of Christ are establishing beachheads for the kingdom of

God in their homes and families, in their places of employment, in their neighborhoods, in their volunteer organizations—everywhere they go, wherever they see a need. And the church supplies these kingdom beachheads with the realistic, reliable and practical means to live in the reality of the kingdom of God, helping us follow the ways of Christ.

But like all organizations, churches are prone to bureaucracy and often become self-serving. Unless we're careful, we forget that the church exists to supply those who are on the front lines. To be faithful to the Great Commission, church leaders must push back at a religious culture that measures success by how large our church is, by how many programs we have, by how popular we are. When a church remembers that it exists to supply followers of Christ with realistic, reliable and practical means to live in the reality of the kingdom of God and establish new beachheads, then it is doing what it is called to do. And it's OK if this doesn't immediately benefit the church organization, because the church exists for those on the front lines.

We are encouraged that there seems to be, in so many places, a sincere stirring, a hungering for the church to become something different than what it currently is. The tired and worn-out models of external success are becoming increasingly less attractive, among all shapes and sizes of churches. There seems to be a persistant virus of holy discontent that is daring to believe that it is actually possible to reenvision what the church can become.

We hope the story of our church adds to this holy discontent and serves as one of many beacons piercing the religious fog and leading to another and better way.

ACKNOWLEDGMENTS

$\mathcal{T}$his book, at its core, is an expression of love between a couple of pastors and their congregation. The people of Oak Hills Church have submitted themselves to many experiments in spiritual formation over the years, and their patience and unwavering encouragement has been a constant source of strength and endurance. This book is their story, and we are deeply grateful for them. The pastors and staff at Oak Hills have carried the weight of this ministry for years, and we would never have been able to make this journey without them. There are obviously too many names to mention here, but you know who you are and you have the scars to prove it. In addition, the elders of Oak Hills, and many official and unofficial spiritual leaders in the church, have never stopped believing in the vision we have been given of inviting people to experience life in the kingdom of God. Here we especially acknowledge and thank Gina, Steve, Dave, Valerie, Ben and Jerry, Caryn, Candy, Andy, Dick and Dan. During the most discouraging days, you never let us give up and never stopped believing in us. That has meant more to us than words can say.

We thank Dallas Willard for his teaching, his availability, his wisdom and most of all for demonstrating that a transformative life with God is indeed possible. We will spend the rest of our lives trying to live up to the foreword he has so graciously written for us.

A special thanks goes to Valerie Harrison, Jenny Jiang, Katie Albert, Abbie Lueken, Julie Lueken and Diane Carlson for reading parts of the manuscript, offering many crucial suggestions and saving us from certain literary death. Thanks also go to Dave Deroos for his help in getting this book started. And since this is our first book-writing experience, we would have been lost without the amazing help of our editor, Cindy Bunch. She patiently put up with our ignorance, foolishness, inexperience and penchant for the absurd, and carefully guided us toward some semblance of coherence. If this book makes any sense, she is largely responsible for it.

We thank our wives, Diane and Julie, for believing in and loving us. This book would not exist without you. We love living our lives with you. We thank our children, Sam, Abbie and Izzie (Mike's), and Holly, Heidi, Helena, Noah, Brooke and Torunn (Kent's, including a son-in-law and two granddaughters). You make us remember every day how precious this life is.

We are grateful for many pastor friends who have influenced us. Thanks to Jerry Worsham for putting up with both of us when we were young pastors and teaching us how to love a church. We will never forget you. Thank you, Dave Johnson, for many unprintable things and for making us laugh. We thank Keith Meyer for connecting us with other church leaders who long for a new way of being the church. We thank Parnell Lovelace for his friendship as he has pastored our sister church, Center of Praise, for twenty years. And to our Folsom pastor friends—Bill, Brad, Chuck, Dennis, Derek, Glen, John, Nancy, Stu and Tim—a big thank you. Your friendship and prayers over the years have helped to make the church in Folsom a unified presence in this community. It is an honor to serve with you.

Thanks also to Donny Jastrebski and Johnny Tofilon, for getting me (Kent) started on the Way. To Ernie Banks for teaching us how to lose. Let's play two. To Vince Lombardi for taking us back to the basics. And now, shut 'er down Mike G. You've earned it.

NOTES

Introduction

p. 16   long obedience in the same direction: Eugene H. Peterson, *A Long Obedience in the Same Direction* (Downers Grove, Ill.: InterVarsity Press, 2000).

Chapter 2: Deciding to Change

p. 31   Lyle Schaller on consumerism: Lyle E. Schaller, *The Very Large Church* (Nashville: Abingdon, 2000), p. 100.

Chapter 3: The Keys to Transition

p. 39   "If Christ is King, everything . . . has to be re-imagined, reconfigured": Eugene H. Peterson, *The Jesus Way* (Grand Rapids: Eerdmans, 2007), pp. 8-9.

Chapter 4: Rethinking the Gospel

p. 63   It was our red pill: *The Matrix*, directors Andy Wachowski and Lana Wachowski, Warner Brothers and Village Road Show Pictures, 1999.

Chapter 5: Consumerism

p. 69   letter to "Gunnar Thorkildsson": Eugene H. Peterson, *The Wisdom of Each Other* (Grand Rapids: Zondervan, 1998), p. 55.

p. 72   "If we are a nation of consumers": Eugene H. Peterson, *The Jesus Way* (Grand Rapids: Eerdmans, 2007), p. 6.

p. 72   "one has laid down the burden of having one's own way": Dallas Willard, *Renovation of the Heart* (Colorado Springs, Colo.: NavPress, 2002), p. 75.

182

RENOVATION OF THE CHURCH

Chapter 6: Setting Aside Ambition

p. 77   "Take heed lest, under the pretense of diligence in your calling": Richard Baxter, *The Practical Works of Richard Baxter*, ed.
William Orme (London: Paternoster, 1830), 4:234.

Chapter 7: Co-pastoring

p. 89   "the prevalence of individualism among ministers and priests":
Henri J. M. Nouwen, *In the Name of Jesus: Reflections on Christian Leadership* (New York: Crossroad, 1989), pp. 55-56.

p. 89   "stardom and individual heroism . . . are not at all alien to the
church": Ibid., p. 56.

Chapter 8: Understanding the Church

p. 104   "Many pastors and lay leaders recognize that they are in a
superficially successful church": Mark Galli, "How to Shrink
a Church," ChristianityToday.com, April 23, 2009 <www
.christianitytoday.com/ct/2009/aprilweb-only/116-41.0.html
?start=2>.

p. 107   "He wants us to establish beachheads or bases of operation":
Dallas Willard, *The Great Omission: Reclaiming Jesus' Essential
Teachings on Discipleship* (San Francisco: HarperCollins, 2006),
p. xiii.

p. 108   "The rise of the missional church is the single biggest development": Reggie McNeal, *Missional Renaissance* (San Francisco:
Jossey-Bass, 2009), p. xiii.

p. 109   "Missional followers of Jesus don't belong to a church": Ibid.,
pp. 19-20.

p. 111   "Should one not rejoice at a full church": Dietrich Bonhoeffer,
in Eric Metaxas, *Bonhoeffer: Pastor, Martyr, Prophet, Spy* (Nashville: Thomas Nelson, 2010), p. 78.

Chapter 9: Spiritual Formation

p. 116   "Our lives become consumed with the idea that": Ronald Rolheiser, *The Shattered Lantern: Rediscovering God's Presence in
Everyday Life* (London: Hodder & Stoughton, 1994), pp. 37-38.

p. 120   "The primary mission field for the Great Commission": Dallas
Willard, *The Great Omission* (San Francisco: HarperCollins,
2006), pp. xiii, xv.

p. 120   "We are far too easily pleased": C. S. Lewis, *The Weight of Glory:
And Other Addresses* (New York: Simon & Schuster, 1980), p. 26.

Chapter 10: Outreach

p. 138   "One of the most notable impressions the literature": Michael
Green, *Evangelism in the Early Church* (Grand Rapids: Eerdmans, 2003), pp. 17-18.

p. 140   "a process of being conformed to the image of Christ for the
sake of others": M. Robert Mulholland Jr., *Invitation to a Journey: A Road Map for Spiritual Formation* (Downers Grove, Ill.:
InterVarsity Press, 1993), p. 12.

p. 141   "seeing all life as a way to be engaged": Reggie McNeal, *Missional Renaissance* (San Francisco: Jossey-Bass, 2009), p. xiv.

p. 142   "The risk of proclaiming God's word is at the heart of evangelism": Henry H. Knight III and F. Douglas Powe Jr., *Transforming
Evangelism: The Wesleyan Way of Sharing Faith* (Nashville: Discipleship Resources, 2006), p. 56.

Chapter 11: Worship

p. 148   "O ever-blessed Trinity": Father Aelred Squire, unpublished
song (Big Sur, Calif.: New Camaldoli Hermitage).

p. 152   "Every aspect of the time we spend together in the worshiping
Christian community": Marva J. Dawn, *Reaching Out Without
Dumbing Down* (Grand Rapids: Eerdmans, 1995), p. 107.

p. 152   Content, structure and style in worship: Robert E. Webber,
Worship Old and New (Grand Rapids: Zondervan, 1994), pp.
149-52.

p. 154   "What I think God cares about is the disengaged heart": Joe
Horness, "Contemporary Music-Driven Worship," in *Exploring
the Worship Spectrum*, ed. Paul A. Basden (Grand Rapids:
Zondervan, 2004), p. 102.

p. 156   "For all of our apparent passion about God": Mark Labberton,
The Dangerous Act of Worship (Downers Grove, Ill.: InterVarsity
Press, 2007), p. 21.

p. 156   "This is the message that is missing in the literature of contemporary worship": Robert Webber, "Blended Worship," in *Exploring the Worship Spectrum*, ed. Paul A. Basden (Grand Rapids: Zondervan, 2004), p. 130.

p. 158   four common movements of worship: Webber, *Worship Old and
New*, p. 150.

Chapter 12: Mistakes

p. 166   "For the future of Christian leadership it is of vital importance":

Henri J. M. Nouwen, *In the Name of Jesus: Reflections on Christian Leadership* (New York: Crossroad, 1989), pp. 44-45.

Epilogue

p. 176   The beachhead metaphor: Dallas Willard, *Renovation of the Heart* (Colorado Springs, Colo.: NavPress, 2002), pp. 15-16.

formatio
TRADITION. EXPERIENCE.
TRANSFORMATION.

Formatio books from InterVarsity Press follow the rich tradition of the church in the journey of spiritual formation. These books are not merely about being informed, but about being transformed by Christ and conformed to his image. Formatio stands in InterVarsity Press's evangelical publishing tradition by integrating God's Word with spiritual practice and by prompting readers to move from inward change to outward witness. InterVarsity Press uses the chambered nautilus for Formatio, a symbol of spiritual formation because of its continual spiral journey outward as it moves from its center. We believe that each of us is made with a deep desire to be in God's presence. Formatio books help us to fulfill our deepest desires and to become our true selves in light of God's grace.